ZERO TO SEVENTEEN

Life Lessons in Story

Sharmay Rose

BALBOA.
PRESS
A DIVISION OF HAY HOUSE

Balboa Press books may be ordered through booksellers or by contacting:

Balboa Press
A Division of Hay House
1663 Liberty Drive
Bloomington, IN 47403
www.balboapress.com
1 (877) 407-4847

Print information available on the last page.

ISBN: 978-1-5043-3153-1 (sc)
ISBN: 978-1-5043-3158-6 (e)

Balboa Press rev. date: 07/27/2015

Contents

Acknowledgements

Heartfelt thanks to my encouraging family, friends and members of "Write On, Door County." This story arose because you believed in me.

Dedication

Gail Marie Cummings September 1953 – May 2015

Introduction

Zero to Seventeen is creative non-fiction, chronicling my life story from ages zero to seventeen. It covers the events that I remember about growing up. My Mom would call them "life happenings." I included a few family stories from before my birth.

"You made your bed. Now lie in it." I heard this cliché often growing up. The result was that I stuck with situations and relationships long after I realized changes were necessary. These words kept me from moving on when a wrong decision had been made.

I remember too many clichés to list them all. Here are several:

"We don't air dirty laundry at our house!"

"What would the neighbors think?"

"Keep a smile on your face and keep a stiff upper lip."

"Don't be like Pinocchio: always tell the truth."

"Behave like a good little girl."

And, of course, the Golden Rule: "Treat others the way you want to be treated."

When I was ten years old, I found out that I had "Pinocchio parents." They lied. That's the truth. That's my truth.

SR

July 2015

Section One

- Lessons Learned

Chapter 1

I held a 1953 high school class ring in my hand. 1953?

My life changed forever when I saw the year on that ring. I had been lied to for all ten years of my life. A sinking feeling grew in my stomach that felt like sucking my heart down into a pit. Parents lie? Yes, I was lied to, over and over. I felt broken inside; a ten-year-old gullible fool sitting in the attic.

Until that moment, I believed Mom and Dad both graduated from high school in January 1952 and were married in May '52. The truth is, my parents graduated from high school in January '53, married in May '53, and I was born in July 1953. They married eleven weeks before I was born. Not *one year* and eleven weeks: just eleven weeks. That's the truth.

That's not what I had been told.

In the attic of our house I was searching for a box that held my treasures. I bumped a stack of boxes and one rattled when it hit the attic floor. I opened it. The rattling noise was Dad's class ring. The

Boy's Tech logo, the year 1953, and the initials DL were on the ring. A quick glance at a January 1953 Boy's Tech High School diploma and purple High School Letter and I knew this box held my Dad's treasures.

It took a split second to realize I was related to a bunch of frauds. Not just my parents, but grandparents, aunts, uncles, friends... everyone. My family members went along with the lies. Mom and Dad had just celebrated their eleventh wedding anniversary. I was ten years old. They were really married ten years. Everyone lied! Did they think I would never find out?

I wondered what I should do. Do I climb down from the attic and go on about my happy-go-lucky life, as if I never seen the contents of Dad's box? Do I confront my parents and ask about the ring? "Hey, Mom and Dad, what's up with the '53 class ring and diploma?" I wasn't deliberately looking through attic boxes. I bumped a box that rattled when it fell. I investigated. And then Mom was at the attic door.

"Sharmay! What are you doing in the attic? Who said you could go up there?" Mom shouted.

"Looking for my box of treasures! It's been missing since we moved." I stuttered.

"What fell? Are you going through boxes?" Mom said this as she climbed the attic steps. There I sat holding Dad's 1953 class ring. The open box was on the floor in front of me.

Mom said, "What are you doing with your father's box? Put that away. You know it doesn't belong to you."

"I bumped it off the stack. It rattled and I checked to see if something was broken." We glared at each other. I looked directly at Dad's class ring then tossed it back into the box, closed the lid and pushed the box behind me, out of Mom's reach. I turned and grabbed my treasure box. "Got it, see?"

"Don't go snooping through other people's stuff." Mom returned to the kitchen as I climbed down the attic stairs and went to my bedroom.

Later that night, after I was in bed, I heard Mom tell Dad about me looking through his box in the attic.

Dad sneered, "She what? Oh, that's just great. Great. Now we have a snoop. Was she snooping around all over the attic?"

Mom replied, "No, I just saw her with your box open. She looked at your class ring, looked directly at it, turning it between her fingers then she then looked up at me. I'm sure she already looked at your diploma. She didn't even try to hide what she was looking at as she closed your box. Then she pushed it back towards the wall, behind other boxes." Mom tattled on me.

"I'll take care of this," Dad replied.

I couldn't hear anything else that was said as they walked away from my bedroom towards the kitchen. I wanted to run away. My heart pounded really hard and it was difficult to swallow because my throat was so dry. I turned over in bed facing away from my bedroom door and pulled the covers over my head.

Dad opened my door a few minutes later. I pretended to be asleep. I'm sure he knew I was faking. He turned to leave my room without disturbing me.

I couldn't keep quiet about what I had found. I uncovered my head and said in a low voice, "So, Dad, what's up with the '53 class ring and '53 Boy's Tech Diploma?" I couldn't believe I actually said that. It sounded just like when I thought the words in the attic.

"What did you say to me? What DID YOU SAY?"

"You heard me. '53 ring and diploma, not '52."

"We are not going to talk about this."

"Get real. This is my life too."

Dad shouted, "I said we are not going to talk about this. GET IT? I said it was 1952 and that's it."

"It's a cover up. We live lies. Big fat lies. My whole life is a cover up."

"Just shut your trap. We are not talking about this subject. Ever!"

"So then I become a liar too, like the rest of our family?" I retorted.

"Do NOT talk to me like that. Lower your voice and SHUT your mouth before your sister or brother hear you. You need to set an example for them."

"An example of how to live a lie? Someone should hear me, SOMEONE SHOULD!" I shouted. "You and Mom are liars!"

Dad growled, "Shut your mouth and don't bring your mother into this! Decisions were made years ago. I stand on my decisions. This is our life, your mother's and mine, and *we* decide how to live it. I will not have you, the snoop, ruin everything."

"A snoop? That's what you think I am? A snoop? And I 'ruin everything'? Well, you are a big freaking liar. A BIG FREAKING LIAR!" I repeated, enraged. "GO AHEAD live your phony life your way!" I reached over and slammed my bedroom door and the whole house shook.

Dad stomped down the hallway and I heard the back door hit hard against the wall when he pulled it open. Then the screen door hit the outside of the house on his way out the door. Good that he

7

is gone, that big phony, I thought. We live a big lie and Dad believes the lie is the truth because he said so. My whole life has been a lie. And I have been ordered to live the lie.

With a smirk I wondered what the neighbors would think. Us "airing our dirty laundry" by speaking the truth? How awful.

Apparently, I did something bad by looking in Dad's box and didn't even know it at the time. I was curious; just curious. And geez, if there was something so secretive up there, why wasn't it hidden in a safe place instead of in front of everything else in the attic? I had normal curiosity. That was my defense. I created a defense for something that happened in my own house. I spoke up. I confronted Dad, the big self-righteous liar.

The subject was never brought up again. Never.

Chapter 2

My Great Auntie May was my Grandma Lucille's younger sister and my mother's best friend and mentor. Auntie May was known to most people as Auntie May. Friends, business associates, customers and all family called her Auntie May. Mom always called her Auntie May. Mom and Auntie May both worked in downtown Milwaukee and took the bus to and from work together. Auntie May created my name, Sharmay. Here's how my unique name happened.

In 1934, my Auntie May was reading a book with a character named Sharleen. When her sister, Lucille, had a baby girl, Auntie May convinced Lucille to name her baby Sharleen May. Fast forward to 1953 when I was born. Auntie May combined Sharleen May into the name Sharmay and convinced my Mom, Sharleen May, to name her baby girl Sharmay.

Growing up with the name Sharmay created many embarrassing moments when I wanted to sink out of sight under my desk. On the first day of school during roll call often teachers commented,

"Oh, Sharmay, what a pretty name." Everyone in class would look at me as I turned red and my ears burned with embarrassment. This happened more times than I could count. It took me until college to appreciate my unique name. By then I had told the story many times of being named after my Mom, Sharleen May, all due to Auntie May's creativity. Being named Sharmay turned out to be great!

Preston was originally my Dad's middle name: David Preston Leetch. Sometime before Dad's graduation from high school, he changed his name to David Lee Preston. Apparently, he didn't want Leetch on his high school diploma. However, his name change was after his class ring and luggage with monogrammed initials were ordered. His luggage shows the initials DPL, and his class ring's two initials are DL. Wait until the last minute to change your name and mess up monogrammed items forever. Way to go, Dad!

When I was a little girl, Grandma Lucille told me the romantic story about how Mom and Dad met during a high school football game. They were both seniors attending different Milwaukee high schools. Mom, Sharleen May Winter, went to Washington High School and was the drill team leader. Dad, David Preston Leetch, went to Boy's Technical High School. He was the bandleader and played trumpet in Tech's Marching Band. When they started going steady, Dad gave Mom his high school class ring to wear: the same

1953 class ring I later found in the attic! After graduation from high school during January 1953 they married in May 1953.

After their marriage, Mom and Dad lived with seven of my mother's extended family members in a five-bedroom farmhouse on the corner of North Avenue and 101st Street in Wauwatosa, WI. The farmhouse was shared with my Great-Grandparents Lillian and Walter Kamp, Grandparents Lucille and Ray Hillyard, Grandma's younger sister Auntie May, her husband Uncle Tony Hauke, and Mom's teenage brother, my Uncle Walter. That was one full household!

Three duplexes were under construction across the street on North Avenue for the families to soon live in. Family and friends were helping the construction crews to finish the duplexes as soon as possible.

In July 1953, Mom was 9 months pregnant with me. I was told it was a hot, humid summer in the days before homes had air conditioning. Some businesses had air conditioning, and they were very popular places when the weather was hot and humid. The story goes that Mom and Dad went into an air-conditioned movie theater the evening of July 19, 1953. That night, Mom didn't sleep well for many reasons, which could have included the weather, being in early labor or because she lived in a house with *eight* other people.

The morning of July 20, my Dad left for work around 6:30am, as usual. Shortly after he was gone, Mom's water broke and intense labor began. She had a frantic time trying to reach my Dad who rode the bus to work. Those were the days when most folks did not have telephones, and the folks who did have telephones had party lines. Everyone knew everyone else's business: they just had pick up the phone to listen to others' conversations.

Grandma Lucille interrupted a party line conversation and demanded to use the phone line for an emergency call. She was able to reach Dad's boss at work and leave a message for Dad that Mom was going to the hospital to have their baby (me!).

Mom was driven to St. Joseph's Hospital by my Great-Grandparents, who dropped her off, and returned home.

They returned home?

Yes, Mom was alone at the hospital to have her first child. They didn't drive to my Dad's workplace and pick him up to take him to the hospital either. Great-Grandpa and Great-Grandma went back home. Auntie May was told, "No, we did not drive around the city to try and find David. He can take the bus to the hospital. We are not a taxi service."

Mom was admitted to the hospital at 7:30 a.m. and I was born at 8:20 a.m. What a speedy labor and delivery! As expected, Dad took a bus across town from work to the hospital and arrived several hours after I was born.

The summer heat blistered on after my birth. As a newborn I wore cloth diapers enclosed in rubber pants, T-shirts with long sleeves that covered my hands and fingers, and on top of all that clothing, I needed to be wrapped in swaddling blankets. I also needed to be sheltered from the drafts of the oscillating fans that were attempting to move the hot, humid air around the house. Apparently my family didn't want me to catch a cold from the drafty air. Baby pictures show me all bundled up like it was frosty out during a hot, humid summer!

Chapter 3

A Betsy-Wetsy doll was a gift on my third birthday. Betsy and I went everywhere together. Mom and Grandma Lucille even sewed matching clothes for Betsy and me. Betsy's doll blanket was the same material as the blanket on my bed. Betsy slept in her own wooden cradle on the floor next to my bed and I tucked her under her covers every night after saying my prayers. Then I climbed into my "big girl bed."

Soon after I turned three, Mom took me to the dentist. Betsy was with me, of course. Mom and Auntie May had regular dentist appointments but their teeth were old. Why me, I wondered? I was a kid. There was a funny smell everywhere in the dentist office too, a spicy medicine smell. I can smell the dentist office just thinking about it!

After what seemed like a long time from a three-year-old's perspective, it was my turn to sit in the big, cold dentist's chair. I sat in the dentist's chair holding Betsy. A bright light was aimed at my face, and my dentist looked in my mouth. I started screaming hysterically. My screams hurt my own ears.

My dentist completely ignored my screams and concentrated on Betsy's mouth. He kindly explained to my doll what he saw in her mouth. He talked to her like he could open her mouth and pretended to look at her teeth. I heard what he said to Betsy and I sort of understood why he wanted to look in my mouth.

Talking to Betsy and explaining the procedure helped calm me down. Until he used metal instruments and poked around in my mouth. I started to cry again. I wasn't hysterically screaming anymore; I just cried and cried until his exam was over then I climbed onto Mom's lap and cried some more.

It turned out this was the first of many dentist visits. Back in the '50s there wasn't much concern for how "the child" felt about what happened to her teeth. My primary molars did not have any enamel on them and were decaying. The lack of enamel was inherited. I had huge cavities in most of my teeth, even though Mom helped me brush my teeth every night. The dentist covered several of my teeth with metal caps. Other teeth were pulled and metal spacers were clamped to surrounding teeth, as placeholders, until my permanent molars were in. Betsy got me through some scary times in the dentist chair. We became best buddies.

Grandpa Ray, Grandma Lucille's second husband, had a heart attack during one of the times I was at the dentist. Mom and I missed the ambulance driver taking him out of the house; we only saw the ambulance leaving our street. Grandma borrowed her parent's car to follow the ambulance to the hospital.

At this time, heart attack victims were coddled and told not to exert themselves should they survive their hospital convalescence. Grandpa Ray lived. He was required to quit his job which, in the belief at the time, would have overworked his damaged heart. He never drove a car again.

When it looked like he was going to keep living, Grandpa got a less stressful job, working three PM until midnight, as a proofreader at the *Milwaukee Journal©*. He "put the paper to bed" before it went to press for the morning. I was told that this proofreading job brought meaning back to his life.

At my young age, even I figured out that it was good that Grandpa got out of the house and was doing the "right" thing by going to work. I didn't realize people worked to earn money to live. I only understood that people should be working, not, "sitting around the house daydreaming like a lazy bum."

Usually, Grandpa took the city bus to and from work. Sometimes, if Grandma Lucille needed to go to the bank, she would borrow her parent's car, a 1952 Nash, and drive Grandpa to work. If I took a nap "like a good little girl," when I woke up I was invited to ride along with Grandma when she drove Grandpa Ray to work in downtown Milwaukee. This drive also included stopping at the bank where there was a tall, green and gray marble "bubbler" where I needed to be lifted up to drink water as it "bubbled" out of the water fountain. Drinking out of the bubbler was the best part of ride.

After Grandpa's heart attack Grandma increased to full-time work at Johnson's Flower Shop. Grandma Lucille had been working part-time at Johnson's for as long as I could remember. Her working outside the home was a controversial situation for our family. Women "should" be at home taking care of their family. Men worked and supported their family. Those were the determined roles. After Grandpa's heart attack, Grandma supported her family on her income. Grandma Lucille loved working with flowers and providing fresh flower arrangements for her customers.

Mom and I would walk down North Avenue to visit Grandma at work. Mom wanted me in the stroller because it was a long walk. I thought that strollers were for babies. I wanted to walk and would try to climb out of the stroller as she was pushing it down the sidewalk. I remember yelling, fighting and a lot of tears.

Eventually, we came to an agreement, if there is such a thing as an agreement between a mother and a 3-year-old child. I would ride in the stroller when there weren't any sidewalks and we needed to walk on the edge of the road. When we got to the streets with sidewalks I could climb out of the stroller, without any help, and walk alongside it. I had to either keep my hand on the stroller or hold my mother's hand or her skirt.

We often met mom's high school girlfriends along the walk. Ruth, Joy and Pat are the friends I remember. They would walk along to Johnson's Flower Store and we would stop at a drug store for an ice cream soda along the way. Other times, we walked along the Menomonee River Parkway and Mom would bring a picnic lunch for us. It was a big event to put a tablecloth on a picnic table and spread the food for us to eat.

Mom sat at the table talking with her friends and I would run around to the swings and slide and play by myself. Sometimes Uncle Walter would drive by in his car with his teenage buddies. He would beep the horn and wave. If he had time he would stop and push me high up on the swings. I loved the swooping feeling and air blowing on my face when swinging.

Chapter 4

I was helping set the table for dinner and climbed onto a chair to get the glass salt and pepper shakers off the kitchen counter. I was off balance as I jumped off the chair. I fell, breaking the saltshaker, and landed on the broken glass and salt. My right palm and wrist were cut and needed stitches to close the wounds. I screamed and screamed. Salt burned my cuts.

Grandma Lucille and Grandpa Ray drove me to the emergency room. Grandpa carried me down the stairs and out to the car while I screamed in his ear. I screamed during the car ride all the way to the hospital. The doctor in the emergency room threatened to tape my mouth shut if I didn't stop screaming.

I must have stopped screaming because I do not remember a Band-Aid over my mouth. However, Grandpa Ray became deaf in his left ear and he blamed it on me screaming in his ear that day. I still have the scars on my palm and wrist to remind me not to jump off a chair holding a glass salt shaker. Lesson learned.

When I was 4 years old, Mom went to the hospital and came home with a crying baby. My sister was born. To help me feel special, or maybe to get me out of the house and away from the crying baby, Dad and I went for a walk. I pushed Betsy in her pink doll buggy. I was happy to be with my Dad.

When we started on our walk, big fluffy clouds were in the sky. Then the sky started to get dark and cloudy like it might rain. We were about three city blocks away from our house when we stopped at a sidewalk stand for a special treat: ice cream! Thunder started to rumble as we were handed our ice cream cones.

We sat at a picnic table to eat. My ice cream was melting and dripping down my hand. I tried to eat my ice cream fast. The thunder got louder with cracking booms. I was scared to be outside during a thunderstorm because I might get struck by lightning and die! The thunder got louder, and my ice cream dripped onto my dress. Dad helped me with the drippy ice cream cone problem by eating the rest of it!

It started to rain, and we ran under the awning of the ice cream stand. We got wet even standing under the awning. Dad picked me up with my doll and buggy, and as he hugged me close to his chest, he started to run home. That was fun! Dad was carrying me, my doll and buggy and running home in a thunderstorm! We made it home safely, although we were dripping wet. Dad even poured water out of my doll buggy. Dad and I changed into dry clothes, and Betsy needed dry clothes too.

Soon after this rainstorm everything in our apartment was packed up to move across Milwaukee to 71st Street and Florist Avenue. Mom and Dad were very excited because they had bought their first house. We needed a bigger house because the baby crib did not fit in my bedroom. My baby sister slept in Mom and Dad's bedroom until we moved. Good thing too, because her crying woke me and Betsy up.

I knew things before they happened. I don't remember when I learned the word premonition, but I had premonitions as far back as I can remember. I would run to the front window to watch for my Grandma and Grandpa Prestin to drive up. No one else knew they were coming for a visit. I sat near the window patiently waiting to see their car turn the corner and park in front of our house. As soon as I saw their shiny black car, I squealed, "They're here!"

"I just knew you would visit today!" I shouted as I ran outside, waiting for them to get out of their car.

"Of course you knew," Grandma Prestin replied, giving me a big hug. "I was thinking about you as we drove over."

Grandma Prestin always wore colorful necklaces, bracelets, and rings that matched the bright colors of her dresses which could be pink, orange, red, and royal blue, lime green, or even purple. My Dad didn't like Grandma to wear these colors because they were too "flashy." Sometimes she wore matching hats that were "wildly" decorated, according to my Dad.

Years later, I learned that Grandma Prestin worked in an upscale women's clothing store at that time and made many of the hats she wore. She was expected to "dress to impress" the customers and made commissions on her sales. I was in awe learning how she earned what Dad called her "pocket money."

The summer I was nine our family went on a cross-county camping trip. I was excited as Mom, Dad, my younger sister and brother and I set out on our first camping adventure! We drove from Wisconsin to California in our 1958 white-and-turquoise Chevy Nomad station wagon pulling our Nimrod 3-Star pop-up tent camper. We often stopped at historical sites for a picnic lunch or a hike. We sometimes took organized tours. Some nights we camped in National Parks along the way.

Dad was driving us through Yellowstone National Park when I told him to slow down because a bear was on the road around the curve. Sure enough, as we rounded the next curve, a bear was in the center of the road.

Dad asked gruffly, "How did you know about the bear?"

"The thought just popped into my mind," I replied smugly.

A few days later I warned my parents not to stop for the night at a campground along a river in Utah. I just knew there was a problem with snakes at that campground. We camped there for one night despite my warnings. Just as I thought, there were a lot of snakes around. After Dad talked with the camp ranger, and consulted his reptile book, he announced, "The snakes are harmless. If you don't bother them, they won't bother you."

I mumbled quietly, "Sure, don't listen to me. We could have camped somewhere else." Snakes were on the red dirt road as I walked to the pump for water, and they were coiled at the base of the water pump. They slithered around the outhouse. They were in the grass around our picnic table.

Snakes were even under our tent when we took it down in the morning, which meant they were under us as we slept in our sleeping bags.

"How did you know about the snakes?" Dad asked me as we were packing up camp.

My sister answered, "She always knows that kind of stuff! She always knows it all."

I argued, "The snakes just popped into my mind. If you'd listen to your mind, you'd know stuff too."

I became aware that I was the only one in my immediate family that "knew" something in advance of it happening. I often knew about things before they happened. I just didn't talk about them.

Chapter 5

Grandma and Grandpa Prestin lived on Little Muskego Lake several hundred feet away from Muskego Beach amusement park. I begged to ride the wooden roller coaster Sunday after Sunday as I watched Grandpa Wally, Uncle Wally and my dad ride the big roller coaster. Grandpa was in maintenance at the park and he took a test ride every day before the park opened to the public to assure the mechanical equipment was working correctly and safely. Mom said I was too young, so I could only watch as the adults rode the roller coaster.

On the Sunday my family was celebrating my fifth birthday I was finally invited to ride the roller coaster. What a day! My first ride was in the back car because I thought it was safer. My second ride was in the front car. I never did decide if I liked the front car or the back car best so I continued to ride coasters twice whenever I could: once in the back car and once in the front. Every opportunity I had to ride a roller coaster was a grand time. Grandpa Prestin took me along for test roller coaster rides until he retired.

I was almost six when my brother was born. My sister was eighteen months old at that time. All three of us kids were in one small bedroom in our 71st Street house. Those first few months living there with a crying baby were terrible. No one got much sleep and I had to get up for school in the morning, exhausted. I learned to sleep holding a pillow over my ears.

Dad, my Uncle Walter, Grandpa Ray and Grandpa Wally started to build two bedrooms and a bathroom in the attic of our house. It seemed to take a long time before I got to sleep upstairs in my own room.

Then several things happened about the same time. The upstairs walls were ready to be plastered, I had my tonsils taken out at a hospital and the wires in our old TV set started on fire.

My throat hurt from my tonsils being taken out, but the plaster smell in the house made my throat hurt more and the smoke from the TV wires burning made my throat hurt worse. Popsicles did not relieve my throat pain. Even Popsicle™ after Popsicle™ did not help. I cried and cried because of the pain.

Grandma and Grandpa Prestin came and picked me up and took me home with them. I got to stay overnight with them for two nights. That is the only time I remember staying overnight at their house. When I came home my throat felt much better and the wet plaster and burning electrical smells were gone from the house. It was over three years until we got a new TV set.

When the upstairs walls were painted, and the lavender and dark purple paint was dry, my bed and dresser were moved upstairs into my very own bedroom. My sister and brother stayed in the downstairs bedroom. I wasn't near crying kids at night anymore! I did not need to share my bedroom either. The space was all mine, and I wasn't even scared to sleep alone.

I walked six city blocks to 66th Street School every school day from Kindergarten through spring break in fourth grade. We lived in a suburban area of Milwaukee and I did not need to cross any busy streets on my route to school. There were cement sidewalks and paved city streets; no mud puddles or wandering off the sidewalks into neighbors yards.

I usually walked with a group of seven or eight kids that lived on my block. The neighborhood kids in fifth and sixth grades led the way for us younger kids so we wouldn't get lost or kidnapped by some stranger offering us candy to get in their car.

I walked to school dressed for the weather. Rainy days were dressed with raincoats, rain hats with big brims to keep the water off my neck, transparent rubber rain boots and umbrellas. In the colder months, I wore a snowsuit, hat that tied under my chin, mittens-on-a-string, a scarf wrapped around my neck and heavy zip-up winter boots to keep me warm and dry. I would be bundled up!

In Kindergarten I thought it was very grown up to wear rain boots or my heavier winter boots to walk to school. When it was raining or there was snow on the sidewalks the boots made sense. When the sidewalks were dry, all the snow had been shoveled off and the streets no longer had water puddles at the curb to jump over, boots were unnecessary. No one else, absolutely *no one* else, wore boots to school. And the school rule was that if you wore boots to school then you were required to wear then on the playground for recess.

I was the only kid at the 66th Street School wearing boots on the playground. I felt like a baby, not a grade school kid, because I wore boots. I made it through Kindergarten without being too humiliated about my boots but I was definitely aware that I was different from the other kids. Mom didn't trust me to avoid water puddles, stay off the snow banks and only walk on the sidewalks.

I could jump over the puddles by the curbs and keep my boots dry. I wanted to stop wearing the boots.

Mom did not agree: "I don't want your shoes ruined. Put your boots on."

"Why do I have to wear boots?" I wailed. "The sidewalks are dry and I jump over any puddles near the curbs. Nobody else is wearing them!"

"Boots will help your shoes last longer. It doesn't hurt to wear them." Mom replied.

"I look stupid."

"Just put on your boots. Get going now."

"No!"

"No?"

"No! I won't wear boots!"

Mom picked up her wooden spoon and I ran out of her reach. She caught up with me in the back hallway. As she swung the spoon towards my "bumbosity," I turned just enough that her spoon hit the wall and broke. I screamed and cried like she had broken the spoon by hitting me too hard. I still had to wear my boots.

I put on my boots and started to walk towards school. Once the group of kids I was walking with got out of sight of our house I said "I forgot something. I gotta run back home. I'll catch up." I ran back towards my house taking a short cut through the neighbor's yard behind our house. As I ran through the neighbor's yard I pulled off my boots and hid them in their basement window well. Then I ran back to join my friends walking to school. No boots! My feet felt light and free!

On the way home from school I ran ahead of my friends, ran into the neighbor's yard and pulled my boots on. I ran back to my friends and finished walking home with them. No one ever mentioned my boots or lack of boots. No one ever asked why I ran into the neighbor's yard and back to join them walking home instead of continuing through the neighbor's yard, across our alley and into my own yard.

I hid my boots in the neighbor's window well many times over the years we lived on 71st St. Once Mom commented that the heels of my boots were not worn down like she expected them to be. "You must have stopped dragging your feet." She knew I used to drag my feet? I dragged my feet to try and wear a hole in my boots so that I didn't have to wear them. Since I was hiding them and not wearing the boots they were lasting longer. Go figure! If the boots didn't wear out I could wear them longer to protect my shoes. That idea sure backfired on me.

It turns out the neighbor lady knew I was hiding my boots. During the summer when I was outside playing, she was hanging laundry in her backyard. I ran over to say hi and see if she had any cookies for me.

"Hi Sharmay! How's your summer vacation?"

"Oh, it's ok, kinda boring. Not much to do. I'm waiting for the Bookmobile™ today."

"I sort of miss you running in and out of my yard on your way to school!"

"What? You saw me?"

"Every time! I always watched you and the other kids walking across the street. Cars rush around that corner. I wanted to be sure you all crossed safely."

She saw me the first day when I ran into her yard wearing boots and ran out of her yard without my boots. She never told my Mom. It was our secret.

Chapter 6

On my seventh birthday I received a red round vinyl suitcase with a blue felt ballerina on the front and a plastic carrying handle. "I'll put Betsy's clothes in here," I immediately thought. When I opened it up there were pink ballet slippers and an empty black shoe bag to keep tap shoes in. "What are these for?"

"They're for you. Do you want to take dance lessons? You could take ballet and tap."

"Dance?"

"Yes, like the dancers you saw in the movie Saturday and the tap dancers on TV."

"Sure. Who else is going?"

"Class is for six girls. You'll meet them at class."

"Okay."

"You'll have to practice. I will order your tap shoes and you'll get them at your first class."

"Practice? Why? Where?"

"In the basement. You can practice in the basement and that's the only place you can wear your tap shoes or you'll wreck the floor around the house. All dancers practice to get really good at dancing. You have long legs, so you should make a good ballerina."

"So if I'd make a good ballerina why do I have to take tap?"

"Both types of dance are offered as one dance lesson."

"When is class? Do I have to go alone?"

"Tuesday after school. I'll drive you there. It's across the alley from Grandma Lucille's house at one of her neighbors."

"Way over there?"

"After class you can walk to Grandma's house. I'll meet you there."

Sure, I was asked if I wanted to take dance lessons but it seemed to me I was already signed up and didn't have a choice. Mom never answered me about who was in the class.

The dance lessons came about when Grandma Lucille was talking with her neighbor across her alley. Dance lessons were in the basement of her neighbor's house. Grandma arranged for me to be in the next beginner dance class, which started in September.

The sign in front of the house said "Harrison's Dance Studio." The first class Mom came with me into the house. We walked into the house and went down the stairs to the basement without ringing the doorbell or knocking. The neighbor lady, Mrs. Harrison, and her daughter were teaching an advanced tap and ballet class. There were several other girls and their mothers waiting for the advanced class to end. I didn't know anyone who was there.

Mom and I sat and watched the dancers doing a tap dance they had performed for their spring dance recital. I thought they were great dancers and the sound of their taps on the cement floor was exciting. I was going to learn to tap dance too!

My new tap shoes were used shoes. One of the older girls was selling them because they were too small for her. I was disappointed because I expected to have brand new shoes. Within a few minutes I realized these shoes already knew how to dance and they just needed to show my feet what they already knew how to do! I liked the used tap shoes. They were perfect for me. I was way ahead of the other new dancers in my class who had new shoes that didn't know how to dance yet. I was sure it was the tap shoes that made the dancer's feet tap with the music, not the dancer that made the shoes tap. That belief carried me through some awkward moments learning different tap dance steps and the correct tapping sounds.

We learned basic tap dance steps to go with music, which was played over and over, as we learned our dance routine. "The Little Old Man with the Green Thumb©" was a song lyric I remember.

34

Dancing was fun and I especially liked making tapping sounds to the beat of the music.

Now about the tapping sounds. I practiced my dance steps in the basement of our house almost every day after school. Tap shoes make noise. Noise disturbs babies, toddlers, and parents. The "Little Old Man with the Green Thumb©" record was played over and over to practice the dance steps. The song got annoying to everyone who was not practicing the dance steps over and over to get them memorized to perfection.

"Could you turn the music down? The baby is taking a nap," my mother pleaded.

I turned the music down so quiet that only I could hear it.

"Could you do the taps on a rug please? The tapping wakes the baby."

I took off my tap shoes and continued to practice the dance steps in my socks with the music so quiet I almost couldn't hear it. I got it. I made too much noise. This was part of "children should be seen but not heard." Now I had to practice dance without anyone hearing my music or the sounds of my tap shoes. I was being silenced.

I started practicing in my second floor bedroom without music or tap shoes. That wasn't acceptable either because when I did the tap-hop steps my hopping shook the house.

"Sharmay, are you jumping in your room?"

"No, I'm practicing dance."

"You're shaking the house. Practice ballet."

Ballet was easy. I didn't need to practice it. I just did it during lessons. I loved to tap and hear the sounds of my feet to the beat of the music. I continued doing the tap routine but no longer hopped or did the turns, which might shake the house too. Practicing dance without music, without tap shoes and without shaking the house? And be good at it too? I needed to be invisible!

I took ballet and tap dance lessons for two years. For our first dance recital I had a sparkly green costume with fuzzy white trim and I had a dancing stick like professional dancers used in their performances. The second spring dance recital was the end of my dance lessons.   After we moved to 49th Court I was given the choice to either continue with dance lessons or I could join the choir at our church.

"I can only drive you to one after school activity. It's your choice. Dance or choir?" Mom asked.

I thought about this choice for a few seconds. Church was closer to our house and there was no cost to be in the church choir. Dance lessons cost money and so did the dance shoes and costumes for recitals. If I didn't cost so much maybe my parents would like me more. My decision was made.

"Choir. I'm going to join the choir."

"I bend over backwards for you to get to across town for dance lessons and now you want to quit dance and join the choir? Sharmay, you couldn't carry a tune if you were paid to! Choir?"

"Yup. Choir. And I can walk there so you won't have to drive me anymore."

I joined the choir to save my parents money and to be with neighborhood friends. I never learned how to carry a tune and sing. I should have continued with dance lessons. At least they were fun!

Around the same time that my dance music was too noisy, and I shook the house when practicing dance, I was also taking flute lessons. Practicing flute, even upstairs in my bedroom with the door closed, still created noise that bothered Mom and Dad and everyone else in the house. My "flute noise" definitely woke any napping kids.

Dad told me, "I need peace and quiet in my house, not some screeching flute. Children are to be seen and not heard."

I didn't understand. At school I was told to practice playing my flute every day. How was I supposed to improve if I couldn't make any sounds out of my flute? Dad played trumpet in High School. Did he learn to play it silently? I needed to practice without hearing any notes come out of my flute. I learned the finger positions for playing the notes without making a sound. I never knew what the notes or song sounded like until I played during my music class at school.

Chapter 7

The summer I was eight, I was allowed to go to Girl Scout Camp for a long weekend. I rode to camp with several other Girl Scouts from my Troop. We arrived on Thursday and camp was supposed to be over on Sunday afternoon. I remember being worried that Mom wouldn't be able to find the camp and pick us up to bring us home on Sunday. Mom assured me she had the directions and a map. She would be there!

We were to sleep in a dormitory room that had ten bunk beds for our Girl Scout Troop. Everyone brought sleeping bags and pillows. I was excited to claim a top bunk. When it was "lights out" that first night I climbed right up and snuggled into my sleeping bag. I snuggled deeper and further down into my sleeping bag and as I was starting to dream…BOOM! I hit the floor with a crash. I had fallen off the end of the bunk bed.

The camp counselors rushed into our dorm room to find out what the commotion was all about. Well, it was obvious that I had fallen off the top bunk since I was on the floor tangled in my sleeping bag.

I jumped up, embarrassed, shouting, "I'm okay. I'm okay!" I wouldn't ever do that again! Well, I wouldn't get the chance to fall off the top bunk again. All the top bunk mattresses were moved to the floor between the bunk beds. No one was allowed to sleep on the top bunks. Every Girl Scout who thought they were going to sleep in a top bunk now needed to sleep on the floor because of my fall. No one at camp talked with me after that. I was the camp outcast and was snubbed big time.

The next morning I sat alone on a bench behind the kitchen building when everyone went on a hike; everyone except me. Being left behind worked out fine for me: everyone else was exposed to poison ivy on the hike! However, that wasn't the end of it.

Soon after everyone had returned from the poison ivy hike, Mom pulled into the camp driveway. What? Mom's here on Friday? Why? Camp runs until Sunday afternoon. I realized Mom being at camp on Friday was not a good situation.

My mother had been called late Thursday night and told about that little incident when I fell off the top bunk bed. According to camp rules, any accident or potential injury, like my fall, needed to be followed up with a doctor's evaluation to be sure there weren't any unreported injuries. Sure, I was bruised but I was usually bruised anyway from biking, climbing trees and other activities. I was fine; embarrassed and bruised, but fine.

Mom demanded an explanation: "How my daughter could fall off a top bunk bed? Aren't there safety bars on a top bunk?" Yes, there were safety rails on the sides of the bunk beds but not across the bottom of the bed where I fell out.

Then Mom started complaining that I had to now sleep on the floor. And if me sleeping on the floor wasn't enough to complain about, when she found out everyone had gone on a hike and I was left alone in the camp, she demanded an explanation.

"Why was my daughter left by herself? Isn't there a system to be sure every person is accounted for before leaving on a hike?" I was glad to finally get in the car to go home.

Unfortunately, because I went home on Friday morning I was never able to redeem myself for falling off the top bunk and causing the ruckus. Later that year, I sold the most Girl Scout Cookies of all the Girl Scout troops in our region. Still, no one would be my friend. I was a Girl Scout outcast. When I was given my Girl Scout Badge for selling the most cookies, it was at the same event that the rest of troop got their badges for their completed camp projects. All the clapping and cheering was for the camp participants. Not for me selling the most cookies.

We moved to a new house during fourth grade and I did not join the Girl Scout Troop at my new school. I was glad we moved, giving me a reason to escape from my Girl Scout Troop. I was the Girl Scout drop out.

Section Two

■ Lessons Learned

Chapter 8

I was nine, in fourth grade, when we moved to a new house. I was not included in my parents' plan to move because, at that time, kids didn't need to know their parents business even if it involved a change to a different school.

A new school? Yikes! Here is how this change happened.

The Monday after Easter, during our spring break from school, my sister and I had dentist appointments to have our teeth cleaned. Or so I thought. It was a little strange that Mom gave me a red "vitamin" pill to take with breakfast that day. But heck, Mom said, "take it," so I did. I almost fell asleep in the car on the drive to the dentist office, which was weird for me. I rarely fell asleep when we drove anywhere.

When we arrived at the dentist's office my sister was immediately taken to have her teeth cleaned. Mom and I sat in the dentist's waiting room and started to search for hidden items in the "Highlights" magazine monthly picture challenge. I didn't even have time to find one hidden item before I was escorted to the dentist's chair in a room that I had never been in before. I assumed that I got to go to a special room because my sister was in the teeth cleaning room. The dentist was going to take care of both of us at the same time. We would get home faster!

The dental assistant clipped a paper bib over my chest; then held my head and shoulders tight against the dental chair. The dentist immediately stuck a needle in the roof of my mouth over and over. I couldn't turn my head or move away from the needle sticks. I cried and cried. My mouth felt really weird and then went numb. This was the first time I had any shots in my mouth. I didn't have any idea why this was done and then I realized Mom was sitting in the room with me. She didn't say anything; she just sat there looking at me.

Permanent teeth were pulled out! The roots were huge and covered with blood. What a shock! No warning, nothing, just two yanked out teeth. Then long strings of stinky clove oil-soaked gauze were pushed into the toothless holes and cotton rolls were stuck in my mouth for me to bite on to stop the bleeding. I looked like I had two bloody cigarettes hanging out of my mouth when I walked out of the dentist office in shock.

Later, I heard Mom talking with our neighbor and found out the red pill I was given at breakfast was not a vitamin; it was a tranquilizer to calm me down. I was drugged to have teeth pulled out. I also overheard how it was the dentist's idea to not to tell me the plan. My parents went along with the surprise "for my own good."

I had experienced mouth abuse. I was done crying and had moved to anger. No one cared that I was mad and my teeth were gone forever. They thought I was just a kid and didn't need to know what was going on in my mouth. My immediate problem was, how was I going to eat my Easter candy?

We arrived home to the telephone ringing on the kitchen wall. Mom picked up the receiver and got upset, almost hysterical. Then she made several phone calls and I heard what was going on.

We needed to move out of our house immediately; like that day, immediately.

We were moving out of our house?

The buyers needed to move in before Friday. It was Monday. What was the rush? The buyer's house was in the path of the new freeway and construction was running ahead of schedule. Their house was scheduled to be torn down on Friday. This led to chaos at our house!

First, I unexpectedly had teeth pulled and now we were moving out of our house. The whole selling the house and moving situation did not include informing us kids that this was going to happen. These were two life-changing surprises for me in one day.

One hour after the phone call, the movers showed up with a semi-truck sized moving van and ten men started to pack and move our belongings out of the house. While all the packing was going on, I tried to overcome the shock of having 2 teeth pulled, and I cried because I was not able to eat my Easter candy.

The moving men packed and moved all of Dad's woodworking equipment out of the basement. They went to the kitchen, emptying the refrigerator and cabinets. Then the refrigerator and stove themselves were taken out to the moving van.

Another team of packers arrived and began to empty out the attic storage area. There was no escape of the chaos because my bedroom was the next stop for the packers. In a flash, my closet was emptied into a big packing crate, the drawers of my dresser were removed and everything and I mean EVERTHING from my bedroom was loaded into boxes and carried to the moving van.

When my room was empty I went downstairs where Mom and Grandma Lucille were still packing up Mom's "personal" stuff in my parents' bedroom. I overheard Mom say, "No stranger is going to touch my things!" As fast as she had her belongings packed in boxes, the movers carried the boxes out to the moving van. Then her dresser drawers, her big dresser and mirror were moved out too.

I was amazed at what a team of packers and movers could do in one afternoon. The rooms sounded hollow when I walked around our empty house.

After the house was empty, cleaning and painting crews arrived. We went to Grandma Lucille's house to eat supper and we slept in sleeping bags on her living room floor. It felt a little like camping, only in Grandma's house instead of our tent.

The next day, Tuesday, we stopped at our old house and it looked like we had never lived there. Every room was sparkling clean and freshly painted in new colors. My lavender and dark purple bedroom was now yellow. Yellow! I was not impressed.

That was the last time I was inside the house. The new folks planned to move in the next day. Their kids would be starting at 66th Street School on Monday, instead of me going back after Spring Break.

We no longer lived on 71st Street. I felt like I didn't belong anywhere and my mouth hurt this whole time because I had two teeth pulled the *day before*. I was going to start at a new school on Monday with gaping holes where my teeth used to be.

While the packers and movers emptied our 71st Street house there was another crew at our new house on 49th Court painting all rooms the same colors they were on 71st Street. What a surprise! Also, by the time we got to the new house on Tuesday, the moving van was almost empty. The movers had unloaded our belongings and put everything into the rooms where they belonged. Even my clothes were hung in my new closet by the time I got there.

However, the movers did not unpack Dad's woodworking tools. We heard about that for a long time whenever Dad was looking for a tool and couldn't find it. He was angry about his tools not being in "their place."

The first day at Clara Barton Elementary School was scary for me. I was never in a situation before with so many new faces. I didn't know anyone. Even though there were kids in my class from our new neighborhood, I hadn't been at our new home long enough to meet the neighborhood kids.

The surprises continued to come when I discovered that my 4th grade teacher was a man! Up until then, my teachers had been women, and mostly old women, it seemed to me. I didn't even know men could *be* grade school teachers. Anyway, the very first day I was challenged to show the class how to do the "new math" division method I learned at my old school. The "new math" division was the next math assignment my new class was going to start to learn.

So it was the fourth grade math wizard and me. We stood side by side at the chalkboard ready to start our math division speed challenge for the whole class to see. The fourth grade math wizard, doing the division the "old" way, and me, doing it the "new" way. Geez! Nothing like being put on the spot and tested in public on my first day in a new school!

As the timer started, we both wrote the problem on the board. We were doing the math as fast as possible, writing everything on the chalkboard. We finished at the same time. However, I missed putting the chalk on the chalk tray and it fell to the floor. Since I had to pick the chalk up, officially, the wizard was done faster. At least all my new classmates knew I could do math fast and use the "new" division they were going to learn. It sure was a bummer about dropping the chalk, though.

Later that day, our class was outside for recess and my teacher put the math wizard and I to another challenge. This time it was who could jump Double Dutch Jump Rope the longest without stepping on the jump rope. It ended up being me. I won! I ran in and started jumping when the double ropes were already in motion. I won!

Then there was a kickball challenge during gym class. I won that too. I could kick the ball the farthest and run to base the fastest. I even beat the 4ᵗʰ grade boys by kicking the ball further than any of them. I held my own against all the new kids. I didn't know I had it in me to do that. Whew! And no one mentioned the gaps in my teeth, either.

A few days after we moved into the new house, I had a premonition. I felt that my great-grandma, Mummy, had died sitting up in her bed. Blabbermouth me, I announced to my parents "Mummy died sitting up in bed."

Mom and Dad looked shocked and started to scold me when the telephone rang. It was Grandma Lucille calling and crying as she told us Mummy *had* died. Just like I knew, she was sitting up in bed when she died. Grandma, standing at Mummy's bedside, handed her a glass of water. Mummy swallowed and died. She just tipped right over in bed. "Right again!" I thought. Then I started to cry because Mummy had died and I knew it before we got the telephone call.

My parents got irritated with me for talking about things that popped into my mind and hadn't happened yet. By then, I had learned these were called premonitions. I was told in no uncertain terms by my Dad, "Keep those thoughts to yourself. It's not normal. You shouldn't know about things before they happen. I don't want to hear about this kind of stuff anymore." My feelings were hurt. I thought everyone knew about things before they happened. I wanted to use my ability to see the future to tell other people.

Grandma Prestin said, "Honey, you're just like me. You've got that sense of knowing things before they happen. That's special, honey, and people who don't have that special sense are scared by it. You can tell me about stuff anytime. I'll understand." Grandma Prestin was so sweet to me.

I was not allowed to talk about the premonitions when I had them, so after the event happened, I *had* to say, "I knew that." Well, that wasn't acceptable either. I was accused of making it up.

My sister yelled, "She's just making it up again. Dad, stop her. Sharmay's making stuff up again!"

I heard this, or something similar, time after time from my sister. Dad sternly reminded me, "Remember? Do. You. REMEMBER? I told you to stop that. I don't want to hear about you knowing stuff before it happens. Just stop it! DO YOU REMEMBER NOW?"

"Yes Dad," I said. "I remember. But...."

Dad interrupted me. "No buts about it. Stop it now or else....!"

Dad always had the final word and must be obeyed or else..... well, I didn't really want to find out what the "or else" was.

I stopped talking to everyone in my family and stayed in my bedroom as much as possible. Mom said, "David, Sharmay's in her room sulking again." No response from Dad. Mom pleaded to Dad "David, please do something about her!" His terse reply? "She's your daughter, *you* do something about it!"

What? I'm just *her* daughter, not his? He's not responsible? I pondered these thoughts for a while and came to the conclusion that I was just an unwanted person. I told myself to just suck it up and get over it. My family didn't want to hear what I knew when I knew it. If I claimed I knew the information after the fact then I was accused of lying about knowing it beforehand.

I had no reason to talk with people who did not want to hear what I had to say and then didn't believe me anyway. When I was at home I isolated myself by reading in my bedroom or listening to records in the basement and playing bumper pool or pinball. If someone came into the basement I went back to my room. My presence was unwanted and I felt unworthy for my existence. I was a bother to my family just because I existed. Avoidance was my coping method.

Just leave me alone.

Chapter 9

I had been at my new school about one month when I decided to race the school bus home. I wanted to run from school to home and beat the bus. I remember the exact day: May 12, 1963.

The school bell rang, signaling school was over for the day. Instead of lining up to get on the school bus, I started to run down the school driveway in the direction of my house. I ran as fast as I could for several blocks, staying on the side of the road since there weren't any sidewalks (hence the reason we were all bused to school - no sidewalks). I saw the buses pull out of the schoolyard and I decided to take shortcuts across neighbors' yards.

Taking short cuts was a good idea, until I decided to climb up and jump off a four-foot pile of boards in one of the yards. I ran up the pile of boards and jumped down. I almost cleared all of the boards. Almost. Instead, I landed on a board with a nail sticking out of it. The nail punctured my foot. OUCH and double OUCH! No time to stop though or the bus would beat me home.

I must admit the nail injury slowed down my running, but I kept going. I picked up speed as the intensity of the puncture resolved and I got to the bus stop just as the bus pulled away and turned the corner. There sat Dad and Mom in our 1958 turquoise and white Chevy Nomad station wagon. They were waiting for me to get off the bus that I wasn't on and were just a bit angry. That is understating it…they were hopping mad.

A teacher reported that she saw me in the "No Children Zone" next to the school bus loading area. A phone call to my parents notified them that I did not get on the bus and had run off the school grounds. I had been at that school less than one month. Who knew there was a rule that students MUST take the bus home unless a parent had notified the school office that someone was picking up their child that day? Who knew? Well, I found out, that's for sure!

How do I remember the date of this event? My youngest cousin was born that day and my parents were waiting at the bus stop to pick us kids up to see the new baby in the hospital. Dad and Mom were not happy with me. Oh, well, it wasn't the first time they were mad about something I did. It wasn't the last time either!

Dad roared at me, "Whatever made you decide to run home from school? Your mother was so scared she thought someone was kidnapping you and you ran from school to get away from the kidnapper. What were you THINKING?"

"But, but I thought….." I tried to express the excitement I felt to race the bus home. Dad cut me off, shouting, "There you go, trying to think again! Be sure your brain is in gear before your mouth is in action. Don't think out loud. We don't want to hear your thinking. Be sure your brain is in gear before your mouth is in action. Get it?" Dad repeated this to me several times.

Like I didn't get the message the first time he said it. I was devastated. I struggled to speak, to find the right words but all that came out was, "Yeah, sure, okay." I slunk away. What was I was trying to say anyway? That little old me thought I could beat the bus home? Yeah, that was it.

It was only important to me to beat the bus to our bus stop. I never even felt any excitement about the fact that I ran home as fast as the bus. I didn't beat the bus but I was there at the same time as the bus even with a nail puncturing my foot. Now that I think about it, I was pretty awesome running home just as fast as riding the bus would have been.

Later that night, I was sure I was going to die from lockjaw because I never, EVER, told anyone about landing on the nail.

Everyone believed if you stepped on a nail you would die a horrible death from tetanus with your jaw locked shut.

I was also afraid someone might look at the bottom of my shoe for some reason and see the hole in it. I lived (obviously!) and no one ever commented on the hole in my shoe either. But I never tried to beat the bus by running home again. Lesson learned, instilled by the fear of being kidnapped.

The summer after fourth grade, I started organizing my bookshelves and moved the furniture around my bedroom. I was settling in. My new bedroom was at the end of the hall surrounded by the rest of my family's bedrooms. I was not upstairs by myself and I was too close to everyone else in the house. Also, my new bedroom was much smaller than at our other house. I felt better when I had my furniture positioned so I could look out the window into our backyard. Looking out the window offered me a sense of space that didn't really exist in the house.

I could look out my window when I was lying on my bed daydreaming (or wasting time doing nothing, according to Dad). One day in July, I was lying on my bed reading a mystery when I realized I hadn't come across my treasure box of "secret stuff" when I reorganized my bedroom. I looked through my dresser drawers and all unopened boxes in my closet and couldn't find my treasure box.

The box held my favorite turtle pin, real perfume from Mummy, some rocks and other secret stuff. Where the heck could it be?

The attic!

I waited until Mom was outside talking with a neighbor, then I went up into the attic to search for my treasure box. I saw my box on top of a stack of boxes under the attic eaves and crawled over to it. As I was crawling I bumped a stack of other boxes and one of the boxes rattled when it fell. I opened it to investigate. Well, you already know how this attic situation turned out with my Dad's 1953 high school class ring. My life changed forever.

That was the summer I turned ten years old. I was a double-digit age! Birthday gifts included a ruby red birthstone necklace and a blue transistor radio complete with a spare battery and a black carrying case. My special birthday gift was a new 3-speed blue bicycle. A new bike, not a repainted bike from the resale shop.

It must be said again: a new bike! I was excited. Plus, the transistor radio was just like the ones teenagers have. I started thinking of myself as a teenager that year. A ten-year-old teenager.

I desperately wanted to show my friends my birthday gifts. I was intent on escaping from the house on my bike, with my transistor radio in the bike basket. Wearing my necklace, of course. I ran out of the house and tried to get on my new bicycle as fast as I could.

Nope. Dad exploded out of the back door, slamming the screen door into the side of the house with a BANG. He ran and grabbed my bike which stopped me in my tracks.

Dad yelled, "Take that necklace off *now*! Only tramps wear jewelry with shorts and tee shirts! Get it off now!"

My thought? "What's a tramp and what does that have to do with me wearing my new necklace?" I started to speak but it came out as stammering. "But I thought, well I thought....um, well....I wanted to show my friends..." My heart felt like it was pounding out of my chest. I was too scared to speak.

Dad released the hold on my bike and grasped my jaw firmly with his left hand. His fingers grabbed under my lower jaw, his left thumb pressed my lips tightly together and his right index finger tapped against my right temple. Through his own clenched jaws he yelled, "Be sure your brain is in gear before your mouth is in action! Get it? GET IT?" He shouted even louder to make sure that I did get it. "Brain in gear before MOUTH IN ACTION! I don't want to tell you this again! GET IT?" He reinforced his point by squeezing my jaw even tighter as he continued to tap the side of my head harder and harder.

How do you reply when your mouth is held shut? I just thought, "Yeah, I get it," as I twisted, bent over and pulled away from him. I dropped my bike.

Finally free, I shouted, "Leave me alone!" as I ran up the back porch steps and pulled the screen door open, which slammed into the house with another BANG. I ran through the house to my bedroom and slammed the bedroom door behind me. Pictures rattled on the walls.

Dad continued to yell down the hall behind me, "Get that necklace off! Now!"

I yanked the necklace off and threw it at my bedroom door. I laid on my bed crying into my pillow. As my sobbing subsided, I heard Mom talking on the kitchen wall phone. I pictured her sitting at the table with the phone cord stretched across the room.

Mom said, "David and Sharmay are at it again, another 'occurrence.' I am sure she's in her room for the afternoon. David's in the garage putting her bike away. I don't know where he's headed but I hear the car running. Great. I get to pick up the pieces again. Talk with you later."

I wondered who she was talking with. One of her friends? Or Grandma Lucille or Grandma Prestin? Who knew that these "occurrences" with Dad were going on?

I heard Mom walk towards my bedroom at the end of the hall. She hesitated at my bedroom door then knocked gently. "Sharmay, your father's gone. He just drove away. Please open your door."

Mom's words sounded kind but I could tell she was "exasperated." Exasperated was one of her favorite words. I heard it often, as in, "Sharmay, you are SO exasperating!"

I opened my bedroom door and threw myself back facedown on my bed. Mom turned away without another word and returned to the kitchen where dinner was cooking on the stove.

Promptly at 5:30pm Dad returned home and Mom shouted, "Dinner is ready!" I stayed lying on my bed. After a short pause, Mom shouted, "Sharmay! Come to the table." Just like nothing had happened, the five of us sat in our designated seats, at the designated time and ate dinner. Each of us acted as if no "exasperating occurrence" had happened that afternoon. We were one big happy family! Or so we pretended.

Chapter 10

I wanted to fit in with the kids in our new neighborhood. I was already self conscious about being the tallest girl in school and that summer my "play" shoes became my mother's old bowling shoes. Size 8. The shoes looked huge and they were old two-toned brown Clodhoppers. I was also required to wear little white ankle socks. I was embarrassed to be wearing both.

I was laughed at and made fun of everywhere I went. My girlfriends didn't want to be seen with me. "Don't want to be seen hanging around with the 'old bowl'!"

These girls wore cute, white KEDS or PF Flyers that made you "run faster and jump higher," at least according to the commercials.

The neighborhood boys were relentless too. They shouted across the street at me, "Hey, clod-hopper!" "Bowl much today?" "Have a nice trip?" "Where can I get shoes like that?"

On and on it went for most of the summer until I redeemed myself. I always showed up where the kids were playing and excelled.

Climbing trees? I could climb and jump off the highest branch. Playing baseball? I could hit past the outfielders and run fast enough to get on base nearly every time. Eventually, my bowling shoes were accepted.

Then it was time to shop for school shoes. I did not get to pick out my shoes for fifth grade. I thought nothing could be worse than the bowling shoes, but I was wrong.

My feet were now size 8 ½ and my new school shoes were huge white and black saddle shoes. Of course those little white ankle socks came back, too. Saddle shoes were popular when my mother was in high school *ten years* before that. What was she thinking buying me saddle shoes? Reliving her memories through me?

Dad said, "They are a nice sturdy pair of shoes and should last the whole school year." They lasted longer than one school year. I wouldn't be surprised if those saddle shoes were still be out there in the resale shops!

The summer before sixth grade I again realized everything, EVERYTHING, I did annoyed someone in my family. As soon as Dad walked in the door after work Mom, my sister or brother, and sometimes all three of them at the same time, complained to Dad about something I said or did during the day.

My whistling "noise" could be heard throughout the house. This obnoxious whistling was the straw that broke the camel's back and Dad intended to set me straight and let me know once again that "children were to be seen and not heard."

Dad was intent on straightening out my "awful" way of acting around everyone. "Where is Sharmay? In her room again? Sulking?" He took out his frustrations and disappointments on me. I was his sounding board.

"Stop that noise. Stop whistling. It bothers your mother and your sister and brother too. We don't want to hear that noise. Just stop it NOW." Dad set me straight.

Dad ended our discussion of "behavior rules" by saying, "Now get to the kitchen and help your mother get dinner on the table. It's after 5:30. We need to eat and you're holding up everyone's dinner."

Everything was always my fault; everything. I was born, therefore, *their* life was my fault. There, I finally thought it! Everything that happened in our family was my fault because I was born. They became this family because of me. I was the family victim. Go ahead folks, pick on me! Vent your frustrations at me! I can take it. I am resilient. "I am a rock and a rock feels no pain." (Words from the Simon and Garfunkel song sure helped me out!)

I got it. I was expected to show remorse for my "obnoxious" whistling and "setting a bad example" for my sister and brother. My repressed remorse meant that I had to lie about my feelings. I hung my head, dangling my arms at my side. I stared at the floor.

Mom told me, "You should know better than that and set a good example for your brother and sister. Don't be causing more problems."

The "real" family was my sister and brother. I was just the unwanted burden and "always caused problems." I was trouble all the way around. According to Dad everything I did, or didn't do, was either "trouble for your mother" or "caused problems for everyone here."

During this same time, I was not allowed to play with my sister or brother. According to Mom, "you are too old to play with them. Go find someone your own age to play with. Don't be causing problems with the younger kids. They are too little to understand your games. Go read or something."

My sister was four years younger than me and my brother was six years younger. I was ten and I could have learned how to play with them. Instead I felt like an outsider trying to intrude into my own family. I always felt like an outsider.

Chapter 11

I was supposed to be asleep. Instead I lay in bed listening to radio station WOKY on my transistor radio; the transistor I got for my tenth birthday. Listeners were invited to vote on which song they liked best by the new English rock group, The Beatles. During Christmas Break 1963, I heard the first Milwaukee broadcast of "I Want to Hold Your Hand" and the flip side song "I Saw Her Standing There."

After I heard both songs, I jumped out of bed and ran to the kitchen wall phone to vote for "I Saw Her Standing There." Our teenage babysitter was at the house that night. She didn't stop me from phoning in my vote, but she was angry that I was listening to my radio when I should have been sleeping. She wanted to take my radio away from me.

I convinced her to let me keep my radio and promised not to listen to it any more that night. She agreed and told me to get back in bed. Since this was a first time situation she also agreed to not tell my parents about it.

I lied. As soon as I was back in bed I turned on my transistor to listen for the voting results. I heard my parents' car in the driveway at the same time the results were announced. "I Want to Hold Your Hand" won. I was disappointed and turned off my radio as Mom and Dad walked into the house. Mom immediately left to drive our babysitter home. Dad opened my bedroom door to check to see if I was asleep. Nope, not sleeping, but I pretended I was.

I cost money because I grew out of my clothes and ate food. I was to be silent. Remember the "brain in gear before mouth in action" guideline? According to Dad my thoughts were jumbled and I needed to "get my brain in gear before my mouth was in action." But if I didn't answer fast enough, Dad shouted at me, "Answer me now, will ya?" I wanted to sink into the floor and be unnoticeable.

Instead, I grew taller and taller. I topped off at 68 inches but no one noticed that last inch. I was short waisted, or long waisted, or something that regular clothes didn't fit right. Blouses were too short and wouldn't tuck properly into my waistbands. The tops of my dresses needed to be made longer for the waistline to be at *my* waistline. This was back in the days when most clothes were homemade. I had skirts and dresses made out of old curtains. Stiff, heavy ivory fabric with green leaves on twisting vines. Okay for curtains, but not for dresses.

During the summer I was eleven, Mom sewed me two summer outfits called "Sassies." Sassies were sleeveless tunic tops, almost the length of a dress, with two slits in the front creating a loincloth type of flap, which revealed matching shorts underneath. These outfits apparently met Mom and Dad's criteria for covering up my long legs. According to them, when I wore the Sassies I didn't look so much like a scarecrow, bean stalk, string bean or any of the other names I was called.

That same summer of the Sassies, I wore my trusty white and black saddle shoes with white ankle socks to play in. I also had white shoe polish. Remember the bottles of polish with a puffy ball tip applicator attached to the cover? I was required to keep my shoes polished a bright shiny white. I was allowed to use my Dad's boot polish to keep the black saddle leather nice and shiny.

I tried to wreck these shoes when I wore them walking in the creek behind our house. After being wet they squished and squeaked when I walked, but the saddle shoes still held up through the summer.

It was time for sixth grade school shopping. I pleaded my case for new school shoes. "Even though the saddle shoes still fit, please,

please, can I get new school shoes? Please? I'll keep the saddles shoes to wear for play after school. Please, can I pick out my shoes this time?" I continued to plead for days.

The most promising response Dad gave was, "We'll see, now shut up about the shoes or you won't get anything. Your sister and brother need shoes too, you know. Do you only think of yourself?" I shrugged my shoulders and turned away as I rolled my eyes. Well, yeah. I did only think of me. Who else would care what my shoes looked like? I learned to keep my mouth shut and those thoughts to myself.

Shopping day arrived. I really, really liked a pair of blue slip-on loafers. Slip-on shoes like the teenage girls wore. I was allowed to try them on. They were nice. Even with my little white ankle socks, they were nice. They weren't to be mine though. Instead, mom bought me dark brown suede, tie-on boots.

"These desert boots are the 'new rage'," Mom said. "Now stop complaining about the saddle shoes. You have new shoes to wear."

Well, the brown desert boots weren't my heart's desire of blue slip-on loafers but they were an improvement from the saddle shoes. All was well, until I got home and tried on the brown desert boots to show Dad. Yikes, and double yikes! What a reaction from him.

Dad shouted at me, "Get those ugly things off your feet. Right now! Take them off and return them. You are NOT wearing anything like that to school. You will return those ugly brown boots. Now! While you can still get your money back."

Dad yelled all this standing on the driveway with me standing next to him. Our neighbors were out in their yard and heard the all the shouting about my shoes. Again, I was embarrassed because of what I wore on my feet, my big Clodhopper feet.

Mom and I immediately got into our station wagon to return the desert boots. I had worn the boots on the asphalt driveway to show Dad. The soles were scuffed up and asphalt stones were embedded in the soles too. I was embarrassed to return the boots but Mom got her money back and we left the store. That was my first experience returning a purchase.

"I never want to go back to that store again," I told Mom.

I didn't have new school shoes and we were late for Mom to get dinner on the table by 5:30, which did not go over well with Dad. An argument between Mom and Dad went on late into the evening. It all started over my school shoes and dinner being served late. It was all my fault. Again.

The first day of sixth grade, I wore my old white and black saddle shoes to school. Dad put black heels and soles on the saddle shoes to "spruce them up and give them a different look for sixth grade." At least they didn't squish and squeak anymore when I walked.

For sixth grade, I was not at the same school as my sister and brother due to crowding, or some other administrative issue. I rode a different bus to school, too. This was good for me as then my sister and brother could not report to Mom and Dad about things I did on the playground or riding the bus.

It was my first feelings of independence.

Chapter 12

I had saved money from summer babysitting jobs in my glass piggy bank. It was filled with coins, and a few dollars. One day I was daydreaming about what I could spend my money on. I thought of magazines, makeup and wait a minute…I had enough money saved to buy the blue loafers. It was *my* money. I could buy my own blue shoes!

Now I had to get back to the store that I never wanted to go to again. I didn't tell anyone my plan, which turned out even better than I thought.

The following Saturday, Grandpa Wally stopped at our house to show us his new car. He took me for a ride in his bright red 1963 Chevy Impala convertible. I conveniently had my money along with me, still in the piggy bank.

"Grandpa, could we stop over at the shoe store for a minute? I want to buy a pair of shoes I saw when school shopping. I have the money to buy them right here," I declared proudly as I patted my purse.

We drove straight to the shoe store and I tried on the blue slip-on loafers. My dream shoes. I was fitted with the same pair of shoes I tried on when I shopped with my mother. Let me describe the shoes in detail. The loafers were slip on shoes, with no ties or straps of any kind to keep them from coming off my feet when I walked. They were made of soft blue leather and decorated with a fringe across the top and a small shiny metal buckle near the outside edge. The soles and heels were black and I had metal cleats put on the heels. The real purpose of the cleats was to prevent the heels from wearing down so they lasted longer but I had the cleats put on for the clicking sound when I walked. The cleats reminded me of tap dancing.

The blue loafers even looked sharp with my little white ankle socks. I felt taller wearing my blue loafers. Older too. Not just a sixth grader. The blue slip-on loafers were shoes a teenager would wear and I was only eleven at the time. Cool!

The clerk and I walked to the cash register for me to buy the shoes. I asked for a hammer to smash my piggy bank.

"What are you doing?" Grandpa calmly asked me as I lifted my piggy bank out of my purse.

"I'm going to smash my piggy bank to get my money for the shoes," I answered.

"You shouldn't have to pay for your own shoes," he said.

"Really? They're just what I want and I need them. It's my money, I can buy them!" I said. I was scared I would not be able to get the blue shoes.

"I'll buy them for you," he replied.

"Really, you will?" I burst into tears. "Thank you! Thank you, thank you!

I wore my new blue slip-on loafers home. They were a gift from Grandpa along with my own tin container of blue shoe polish. Dad couldn't argue about my shoes because Grandpa bought them for me. Mom gave me a new pair of white ankle socks. My piggy bank remained whole; I still had my summer earnings *and* my new blue slip-on loafers.

Things I remember about the 6th grade:

I wore my blue loafers every day.

I sprained my right thumb playing first base on our softball team. I tried to catch a line-drive with my right hand and the ball hit my right thumb, bending it backwards. OUCH! After that I never reached out with my ungloved right hand to try to stop a ball. DUH!

I really, really wanted black shoe boots with fur along the top edge for Christmas that year. Black shoe boots were the most popular style that year. EVERYONE was wearing them. If you had shoe boots then you needed to carry another bag to school with your shoes in it. So for Christmas, I asked for black shoe boots and a shoe bag. I didn't get them. My mother did. Well, at least she looked cool!

I was still a dorky sixth grader wearing my brown rubber boots that zipped up over my blue slip on loafers. The zipper was in the center and went from the toes to the top of the boot. They did have a fur edge but old women wore those kind of boots, not cool sixth graders. I wore those boots almost every day all winter long because I wanted to protect my blue loafers so they would last longer.

I was the tallest girl in the school. Most of my clothes (and winter boots!) were hand me downs from someone who was shorter than me. I had a long torso with skinny legs. The hand me downs rarely fit me. Girls could not wear slacks to school. We had to wear skirts or dresses. Even wearing tights was controversial. Ankle socks were normal; knee highs were a bit outrageous too, but were allowed during the colder months. I had very few clothes that were comfortable and fit well.

I carried papers back and forth to school in a blue plastic zippered folder. It was so cold that winter that the folder shattered when I dropped it getting off the bus. Ok, I may have thrown the folder as I got off the bus, but in any case the plastic folder shattered when it hit the ground.

I got very stylish eyeglasses with light blue frames during the sixth grade. I was told the blue frames made my eyes look bluer. The important thing was I could finally read the chalkboard from my desk in the back of the classroom. We students were all seated alphabetically by last name. Preston usually put me somewhere in the middle row. Since I was tall, no one seated behind me could see the board. I was always moved to the back seat of the row.

Acne began during sixth grade and I was allowed to wash my face with Phisohex™ for its antibacterial properties. Then after months and months of no improvement washing with Phisohex™ I was allowed to use Clearasil™ which dried to a pasty brown glop on my skin.

Dad said, "I don't know how you can go out in public looking like that with brown glop on your face." What a blow to my self-esteem. I took his comment personally. It added to my feelings of being a failure and that comment made me even more self-conscious about my skin.

Grandma Prestin started bringing over acne products for me to try which my Dad did not agree with. "Just let her skin be natural,"

Dad told her. I remember she "snuck" me a green mask to dry oil on my face. Grandma suggested I only use the mask when I was in the bathroom so Dad didn't know about it. She also brought me a heat lamp to increase the blood flow to my skin to help clear it up. Grandma told Dad the heat lamp was a reading light so I could see to read in bed before going to sleep. None of these products or actions helped clear up my acne.

Near the end of sixth grade, I was offered a choice of which junior high school I would like to attend. A school counselor told me, "You learn fast and then you move on. You have the potential to be the smartest person in the regular classes at John Muir Junior High or you could be at the bottom of the smartest group of students in the new Superior Ability Program (SAP) at Thomas Edison Junior High." Without hesitation or discussion of possible consequences, I chose being the dumbest person in the smart class.

I ended sixth grade knowing I would be the dumbest person in the seventh grade smart class at Thomas Edison Junior High. I sure wasn't going to tell anyone that I was the dumbest person in the class. But knowing I was the dumbest person in the class added to my low self-esteem. Another failure. I was the dumbest person.

All the other sixth grade kids in my neighborhood were going to John Muir Junior High, but I heard about a new neighbor who was also going to be at Thomas Edison, because her older brother already attended school there.

We lived about three blocks apart on opposite sides of the small creek I walked in wearing my black and white saddle shoes. I don't remember how or why, but we started chumming around together for a few weeks during the summer.

The week after summer vacation began, we decided we would run away from home at night to my grandma's house, which was about six miles away. We planned to sneak into her empty upstairs apartment and live there for the summer.

One night, after making plans to escape to my grandma's house, we both climbed out of our bedroom windows and met along the creek. We dodged car lights and began our trek. After getting about two miles from home, I chickened out and said that if we turned around now we could be back home before dawn. We could climb into our bedroom windows and be back in bed without ever being caught. We headed home.

Except for leaving smudge tracks on the siding below my window, no one ever knew about me almost running away from home. I was scolded for sleeping until noon the next day, but that is all I remember about the event. I didn't see my neighbor after that night. She really was ready to run away and my chickening out disappointed her. I even failed at running away.

Several times that summer I climbed out my bedroom window at night and sat on our picnic table in the backyard. It was peaceful, looking at the stars and just being alone. I had escaped the house! It was also rather risky sitting on the picnic table because it was in the backyard about fifteen feet from my parents' bedroom window. If I had sneezed or made any type of noise I am sure I would have been caught.

I never was caught.

Dad mentioned the marks on the siding below my bedroom window and asked if I knew how they got there. I explained the marks were part of a fire drill. I climbed out my window pretending there was a fire. Then I climbed back in the window. There was no further discussion about the marks but I needed to scrub them off. I made sure I didn't put any new marks on the siding after that.

In 1964 when the movie Mary Poppins© was showing in the movie theatres, I was not invited to go to the movies with my sister, brother, Mom and Dad. I was told I was too old for little kid movies. I was old enough to stay home alone and that's what I did. I was too old for Mary Poppins©? Everyone at school was seeing it with their families. Not me. I stayed home alone.

There I go, using the phrase "everyone" was doing something. If I used the "everyone" word around Mom, she said the typical refrain: "If 'everyone' was jumping off a bridge would you jump too?" Point taken. *Almost* everyone was going to the movies to see Mary Poppins©. I was not. I wanted to be included and to be wanted. I did not want to be considered a burden due to the cost of another movie ticket for a movie they thought I was too old to enjoy. I wanted to be a part of my family.

When I turned twelve, in 1965, I was considered old enough to babysit my sister and brother. How weird was that? I was too old to play with them but I could be their babysitter. When I babysat for the neighbor's kids, I would play with the kids as part of my babysitting job.

I wasn't allowed to play with my sister or brother. I could only watch them to make sure they didn't get into any trouble while Mom and Dad were gone.

Section Three

■ Lessons Learned

Chapter 13

I was so excited to start seventh grade at Thomas Edison Junior High School. I felt like I was on the verge of a new discovery. The first day of school I met Gail. It was her twelfth birthday. Gail was the shortest girl in my homeroom. I was the tallest. We became best friends the day we met. Gail was my new discovery.

Gail and I were so similar it was like we were two peas in a pod. We had a common desperation to be acknowledged and not overlooked because we were girls. Gail's accomplishments were disregarded by her parents because she wasn't a boy. I believed nothing I did was good enough for my Dad because I wasn't a boy.

Gail and I shared a locker and were in most classes together. There were exceptions. I took band class because after my church choir off-key singing, I was too embarrassed to sing in front of the chorus during tryouts. Gail took chorus. During Home Economics, we were separated again. While I had sewing, Gail was in cooking and while I was in cooking, Gail was in sewing.

Gail's motivation to get good grades and join school activities motivated me to strive to follow suit. Gail organized class projects and often was the first person to raise her hand to answer a teacher's question. Sometimes she gave the wrong answer, but that never seemed to embarrass her. If I wasn't absolutely certain I had the correct answer then I did not raise my hand. Remember, I thought I was the dumbest one in the class. I didn't want to offer a wrong answer to confirm to everyone how dumb I was. I never realized that all students were learning new material in every class. I thought my classmates just knew everything and I didn't.

Gail lived south from school and I lived northwest of school; our houses were 3.5 miles apart. Gail's family lived in "The Housing Projects" which, according to my Dad, were located on the "wrong" side of the tracks.

"Dad told me, "I do NOT want you to associate with those types of people."

"Daaadd, what do you mean 'those type of people'? Gail is my friend!"

"They're from the wrong side of the tracks. They're all a bunch of losers. Wouldn't know a day's work if it hit them in the face; drunks, trailer trash."

"What do you mean 'trailer trash'? Gail's Mom and Dad both have jobs!" This was the first I heard the term "trailer trash" and it sounded mean and ugly.

"Where do they go after work? What do they do then?" Dad answered his own question. "Bars, they go drinking at bars, get drunk. And who is home with their kids?"

"Gail and her two brothers are old enough to be home alone," I answered.

Dad seemed opinionated against my friendship with Gail without any valid reason. He never met her parents but he made judgments about their lifestyle. Worse yet, he believed his judgment to be the truth. I wondered where he got those "trailer trash" ideas and what "drinking at bars" was all about. I had never been in a bar or seen a drunken person.

Gail was my best friend and Dad didn't want me to associate with her. Why? Even if I wanted to avoid her how could I? We were in many of the same classes and we were locker partners. Often I wanted to do something after school or on weekends with Gail and this caused friction between Dad and me. I wanted to know how to avoid these arguments with Dad. One easy way to avoid the arguments was to lie about who I was with or where I was going. Lying might not have been such a good idea, but I lied anyway.

After school I would either take a bus home or, if the weather was good, I would walk. Sometimes I walked with other students who lived the same direction as me. I did not enjoy listening to their chatter, gossip and complaints while we walked. I preferred to walk home alone. Walking was quiet, daydreaming time for me. I could unwind from the effects of school and my classmates. It was like meditation before meditation was popular. I craved solitude.

At least once a week after school, Gail and I would go to the Milwaukee Public Library on 35th and Villard. The library was our sanctuary, a neutral location, without parents or siblings to bother us. We would linger at the library doing homework and checking out library books. I risked being grounded because I did not ask permission from my parents to go to the library after school. I felt like a rebel. I had to run home to arrive at the approximate time that I would have gotten home if I had walked home right after school.

Going to the library after school was the beginning of me doing things by myself and not asking permission. I thought it was foolish to ask, "May I please go to the library after school? I promise to be home by 5:30 for dinner." Then I would be asked, "What do you need to go to the library for? Who are you going with? What do you need to do there? How are you going to get home?" What did my parents need to know all those bothersome details for? I needed to go to the library to do schoolwork and I would be home on time. Trust me. Believe me. There was no known reason to not trust me. At least not yet.

This deception about going to the library was a trigger for me. I wasn't trusted and I had not done anything that I was aware of to not be trusted. If I wasn't trusted and I was trustworthy then why should I behave? I might as well be untrustworthy and deserve to not being trusted.

Sometimes I would go to Gail's house after school and call Mom to let her know I was at Gail's. Mom usually had a terse, snippy reply: "Again? You're at her house again? Alright, be home by 5:30 for dinner." She would then hang up the phone. Visiting at Gail's created tension between me and my parents and we often argued about it when I got home.

Gail had two brothers. Chuck was three years older and Mark was six years younger and because they were at home (where they lived!) it caused problems for me. I state the obvious here: they were boys and I wasn't allowed to have friends who were boys. On top of that, they were "trailer trash" boys. Another factor, which was a valid reason for my parents' concern, was that Gail's parents were not usually home from work (or the bars) while I was at their house.

When Chuck got his driver's license, he often drove Gail to and from school. If Gail and I went to the library after school he would pick us up at the library and drive me home. It was exciting to be in a car with a teenage boy driving. The radio was on a rock 'n roll station and we sang along as loud as we wanted. No one yelled at us to quiet down or told me how I sang out of tune.

I got out of the car several blocks from my house so Mom thought I walked home. Of course, I was not allowed to be in a car with an "inexperienced" teenaged driver, nor was I allowed to be with a boy. It didn't make any difference that Gail was in the car too. I just wasn't allowed to be in a situation where I was in a car with a boy. I was not told why, just that I couldn't do it.

Going to the library and/or Gail's house after school and still getting home at my regular time was like living a secret life. I wasn't really lying about what I did or where I went, I just avoided speaking about how I really spent my time. If Chuck didn't drive me home then I would run home. Who knew that running would improve my outlook on life? I could even tolerate Dad!

I enjoyed running. Like walking, I liked running alone too. It was time that I could let my thoughts flow freely with nothing particular to think about. Sometimes creative ideas would just pop into my head, like painting my bedroom furniture purple. There were many days that I wanted to keep running right past my house until I couldn't run anymore, just to see how long I could run without stopping.

I figured out exactly how long it took me to run home so I was on time for dinner at 5:30. I paced myself to run home without stopping. I couldn't be out of breath or look like I had been running when I got home either. I ran in my regular school shoes most of the time; those blue loafers from 6th grade. Sometimes I wore my white tennis shoes from gym class but then I needed to explain why I wore gym shoes home from school.

Keep in mind this was 1965/1966 and aerobic fitness activities were still years away. Running was only acceptable during gym class or for sports activities. I was a girl running on Milwaukee city streets; not a boy. This was a double whammy against me. I lost count how many times drivers pulled over and offered me a ride. Not in the "pickup" sense but as a kind gesture to drive me wherever I was running to. I always refused rides.

The trouble started after several neighbors saw me running and I refused their offer to give me a ride home. The neighbors talked with my parents about me running on the city streets. I was not on the sidewalk where I belonged but running on the streets where I could get killed by traffic. Sidewalks were concrete and hurt my legs. Therefore, I ran on asphalt streets.

I had another "talking to" from Dad to straighten out my new "tramp-like" behavior. "No more running! I will not have my daughter looking like a tramp running on the streets."

"Now runners are tramps too?" I retorted. "I like to run and there is nothing wrong with me running."

Mom sort of stood up for me. "David, just leave her be. She's only hurting herself by running."

I turned and walked away from my parents. When I got to my bedroom I gently closed my bedroom door. Symbolically I shut out my Mom and Dad's weird, controlling behavior. I had developed some grit and found my inner spark. I just didn't know that yet.

I was on a runner's high and even Dad couldn't stop the good feelings I had after running. I continued to run and ignored the neighbors and ignored Dad's opinion of me running. Leave me alone and let me run!

Every summer Gail went to her Grandma's house in Park Falls, Wisconsin, where she worked in the family motel. I thought it was fun for her to get away from her parents and brothers. I didn't realize she was working everyday doing motel housekeeping without being paid for her time. Dad thought Gail was from the wrong side of the tracks and in reality, she worked long hours without any pay!

Without Gail around during the summer, I did a lot of reading and I babysat for the neighbors. It was unusual for someone's mother to be working; most of the kids had stay-at-home moms. If I babysat during the day, it was so the mother could go shopping, to a doctor's appointment or to run other errands. On weekends, I babysat for parents who went to a fish fry or a wedding reception.

I had one regular babysitting job every other Friday night when the Mom and Dad were on a couple's bowling league. That was nice because I could rely on earning twenty-five cents an hour! Sometimes I earned a dollar; more if they stayed out late.

It didn't seem fair that Gail worked during her summer vacation without being paid and I earned money sitting around a house reading a book while the kids I was babysitting slept. I also earned at least twenty-five cents an hour when I worked at my Grandma's flower store. I saved most of the money I earned to buy school clothes and makeup.

Despite Dad's perception that Gail's family was from the wrong side of the tracks, our friendship continued. I was protective of Gail and our friendship. I didn't invite her to come to my house because I didn't want her to experience any prejudice from my parents that may have affected our friendship. Gail's brother Chuck gradually became a good friend too, like an older brother to me. After all, he had to put up with my presence since I was often with his sister. Chuck wasn't a boyfriend type of friend but a friend who happened to be a boy.

Oh my. I had a friend who was a boy! I was starting to have secrets in my life.

Chapter 14

I was excited to get my first report card in junior high. It was the first time I received a separate grade for each class. My homework assignments were all completed on time and my test grades were either B+ or A's in all classes. I knew I was on the honor roll.

Then our report cards were distributed. It showed that I had almost straight A's in all my classes. Something was not right. I had an A in Metal Shop? I was in Home Ec, not Metal Shop. Where was my Home Ec grade?

At about the same time another student with the same last name of Preston let out a yell. He did not have straight A's and was not on the Purple "A" Honor Role. His report card showed he was taking sewing! "What is this? I'm not in Home Ec! Where is my Metal Shop grade?" he shouted. Obviously, our grades were mixed up. I received incorrect grades on my report cards several times during junior high school.

Several days later, we received our corrected report cards and grade point averages. By then the excitement of Honor Roll recognition was over, but I was proud to have earned almost all A's without studying! Me, the dumbest person in our SAP class, earned almost all A grades. Imagine if I studied! I could have earned all A's, and been on the Purple Honor Roll.

I did not have any interest in achieving straight A's. What I earned with my casual study methods was fine with me.

During 7th and 8th grade I was required to take Home Economics class, known as Home Ec. Mrs. Dreyfus was our teacher for all the Home Ec classes and she always called me "Sharma" not Sharmay. On the class roster the line for printing out our names only had so many character spaces and it didn't print the "y" at the end of Sharmay. I told Mrs. Dreyfus several times my name was Sharmay, not Sharma. She never conceded. I was always Sharma to her.

The first semester was cooking and the second semester was sewing. I don't remember anything about the cooking classes, but the sewing classes were great. I learned how to operate a sewing machine, alter patterns to fit different body shapes and sizes and how to sew clothing.

For my first sewing project of seventh grade, I picked out a dress pattern and altered it so my dress would fit me perfectly. I chose a paisley design in bright orange, emerald green and black. I learned how to lay out the pattern so the fabric grain and pattern pieces faced the right direction, and I sewed the perfect fitting dress!

I made three dresses using the same dress pattern. The second dress was a soft brown fabric with white and yellow daisies and the third was my Christmas dress that year which was a dark red paisley fabric, almost like embossed red velvet. I made two blouses by using the dress pattern and shortening it. The blouses were the best length for me and they stayed tucked into the waistband of my skirts!

Finally, I had some clothes that were my own, not hand-me-downs or old curtains. New clothes that fit and were the colors I liked! I wore turtlenecks under the dresses and blouses during the colder months so I could wear them year round. I wore custom fit clothing of my own design. I was way ahead of the times.

The following year in eighth grade sewing class I learned how to set in sleeves, make button holes and put in zippers. My dress pattern was an empire waist dress that closed with a zipper in the back and a zipper in each sleeve near the wrist to make it a tight fitting wrist area. I made the dress out of two fabrics. The top of the dress was a print with small blue flowers and the skirt was a solid royal blue. It fit perfectly. My eyes sparkled when I wore it. I loved that dress.

Chapter 15

Art class was my favorite class. I loved being creative. For a semester-long project during eighth grade I needed a model to use as a guide for several art pieces we would create. Grandma Prestin had painted "Siesta Man" on a 4" x 4" Mexican clay tile and she offered it to me to use as a model for my art projects. "Siesta Man" was an oil painting, created with a tiny brush. A man was sitting on the ground covered with a poncho, his arms are wrapped around his knees, and his head tipped down under a large sombrero taking a siesta. He was leaning against a building with a Mexican pot next to him. I treasured Grandma's hand painted tile.

I drew this Mexican siesta picture many, many times. Sometimes I drew it as a pencil sketch or with crayons, colored chalk, poster paints or water colors, and sometimes with all of these on the same paper. I turned several versions of my drawings in for extra credit in my art classes. My art teachers thought these drawings were good and I was encouraged to try different variations of the siesta picture.

Dad was unhappy with my Mexican artwork for two reasons. First, I copied another person's work (his mother's!). Second, and worst of all in his opinion, I drew a Mexican. Dad informed me, "We are Americans and you will do American art." He tore up and threw away all of the siesta artwork he found in my room. It wasn't American or original so my artwork wasn't good enough. I don't remember what happened to the clay tile or the artwork I tried to hide from Dad. As my Grandma Prestin said, "Your artwork has gone missing, you can create more. Don't let your dad stop you."

I was required to take a foreign language class starting in seventh grade. I chose to learn Spanish. Grandpa Ray grew up in southern California and spoke fluent Spanish. He taught me basic Spanish and I tried to carry on simple conversations with him. Dad informed me, "We speak American in our house." That was the end of Spanish conversations with Grandpa. As a result I did not learn Spanish, German, Bohemian, or Russian. My grandparents and great-grandparents were multi-lingual; not me! I spoke American or else. I never did figure out what "American" really was.

In our English class, we often had a homework assignment to write a single paged theme paper on any subject that used the day's lessons correctly, such as prepositional phrases, pronouns or adjectives. Sometimes we were assigned a subject to write about, but most days we could choose our own topic.

Most nights, Dad read my homework paper and said, "This is junk. Write it again."

"Junk? It's not junk! Let me turn it in the way it is."

"No," Dad, the critique authority, announced. "It's junk. Write it over, start again, do a better job. Get it right this time. If you'd gotten it right the first time you wouldn't need to do it over."

That's my know-it-all Dad, I thought as I turned away in tears to rewrite my paper again (and again and again…).

No self-esteem remained. Of course, at that time, I didn't know the words self-esteem or what they meant. I just knew I was worthless and couldn't do anything right. My artwork wasn't any good because I used a Mexican tile for my artwork model and it was not "American art" so it was destroyed and thrown away. Not just thrown away, but destroyed.

My English theme papers weren't good enough the first time and I needed to write them over and over until Dad would accept a paper as good enough to turn in for my homework assignment. I didn't do anything right. I didn't weed the garden right, hold a hammer right or hold a paint brush right. I felt like a total failure.

I did not push myself to exceed in any of my junior high classes. After all, I was led to believe that I was the dumbest person in class. Why study when everything, and I mean everything, was covered at least twice during class? I understood it and I was bored. And no matter what I did or how good my grades were, they weren't good enough for my dad.

I learned to hold in my feelings and just "keep a stiff upper lip." I was shutting myself down. I felt that I did not have a welcome place in the world. I was worthless, and often I would fly into a rage triggered by interactions with my Dad. Typical teenage behavior that we now know has to do with the stages of brain development. At the time I was shattered. I felt that almost all my interactions with family were related to their desire to control me. I was being challenged to survive my teenage years as a worthless person who was not supported or encouraged.

I needed to face the facts. I was not considered part of the family. My parents, especially Dad, considered me to be the "family troublemaker." Everything I did, or said, was attributed to my attempts to cause trouble in the family. This was not true. I was a struggling teenager. It was not right to label me and then expect me to live up to the role of a troublemaker.

I felt like I lived in an unsupportive environment. No one in my immediate family wanted me to be around and no one cared about me. I felt unloved; a reject in my own home. I just knew deep in my heart that I had to survive until I was eighteen and then I could move out of their house and live on my own.

Many times Mom said, "I don't care what you do as long as you graduate from high school."

Could I accept this was the way it was whether I liked it or not? Yes. Graduate from high school. Apparently that was all that was expected of me. Graduate. Then I would be a worthy person. Happiness would follow after high school graduation.

Chapter 16

During eighth grade, I was home alone one Saturday morning when the rest of my family went grocery shopping. I went back up in the attic to look for the box of Dad's high school class ring. I looked all over the attic and couldn't find the box. I really wanted to find his ring. Now what?

I stood in the doorway to Mom and Dad's bedroom: a place I wasn't allowed to be. I could see that Dad had a wooden jewelry box on the top of his chest of drawers. I went in their room and opened his jewelry box. I saw his class ring right away. I took it and hid it in my school bag. Then I walked back into their bedroom and smoothed out my footprints in the carpet.

I stole Dad's class ring! Is it stealing if it belongs to your Dad and you live in the same house? I was pretty sure if Dad missed his ring he would report it to the police. I took something of his without permission and I violated his private space to get it. He would certainly turn me in to the police and I would go to jail for this. Dad would make me pay for it.

I intended to show off his ring at school. Not a show and tell, but to brag to other girls about it. The ring provided proof that the story about my parents was true. Dad's 1953 high school class ring really existed. I took his ring to school. Dad would never know it had been out of the house.

"Oh, yeah? Prove it! Show me his ring." Demanded one of my school "friends."

"Here, I brought it." Perhaps this was an attempt to feel accepted, like I belonged in the group.

Who was in this group? Girls that had been together during grade school and now were in junior high together as a "clique." Honestly, I felt like an outsider. Because I lived in a neighborhood northwest of school and went to a different grade school I was considered an outsider at "their" junior high.

Good thing I checked for Dad's ring while I waited to get on the school bus. It was missing from my school bag. Fear gripped my belly. How could I have lost the ring? I put it right back into my coin purse after showing it to the "clique" of girls. I rechecked everything in my school bag. No ring.

The logical action was to go to the lost and found in the school office. If I checked at the office then I would be admitting to myself that I lost something important that I wasn't even supposed to have. I stole my Dad's ring and lost it! What did that say about me? I was not going to the lost and found at this time. It was bad enough to live through.

I ran to the school office just as students were allowed to get on the school bus. I had to hurry or the bus would leave without me and I didn't want to walk home that day. The secretary was in the office and yes, she had the ring. Someone turned it in! And here is the scary part, she knew Dad graduated from Boys Tech and wondered if it was his ring. What if she had called Dad about his ring? That would not have been a good situation for me.

I took back the ring and thanked her for holding onto it. Then I had to thank my guardian angels. "Oh, thank you, thank you, thank you!" I prayed as I ran through the hallway to get on the bus that was still waiting for me. All was well. A scary self created situation, but it turned out fine.

How did the ring get from me carefully putting it in my school bag to the school lost and found? I knew I didn't drop it because I had zipped my coin purse and closed my school bag after putting the ring in. I was suspicious for sure. Did someone steal the ring out of my bag and lose it? Or did someone steal it out of my bag and turn it in to the office to try to get me into trouble? It was possible! Not nice, but possible.

That same evening when Dad was gone to a meeting and Mom was in the living room watching TV with my sister and brother, I quickly and quietly returned the ring to Dad's jewelry box. Never again would I steal to show off at school. Lesson learned.

Near the end of seventh grade, I started a two-year feud with Gail. I slammed our locker door closed as she reached to take out a book. There was no reason for my angry outburst. I just did it. Who knows what was going through my teenage brain? Was I jealous because she got a ride to and from school almost every day from her brother? Or was I jealous because she earned better grades then me? Or that she wrote good theme stories in English class and often was asked to read her homework to our class? Or that she could climb ropes and poles all the way to the ceiling in the gym? None of these were valid reasons to slam the locker closed.

Gail continued to reach out to me to try to understand what I was so mad about. I continued to be mean to her. Gail never stopped being nice to me. We continued to share a locker but neither of us held the door open for the other person. Gail slammed the locker door in my face too. Payback, I guess.

I was a mean and resentful teenager. I was unable to continue friendships. If a person reached out to me, I pushed away any attempts at friendship and said mean things to them. Slamming the locker door in my friend's face was just the start of it.

Maybe Dad would like me and not be so mean to me if I wasn't friends with Gail. Perhaps, unconsciously I was trying to be the "good daughter" and had internalized my Dad's rules to not hang around "trailer trash." Maybe I wanted Dad to be proud of me because I listened to his guidance and tried to obey his rules. I had the power over a friend just like Dad had power over me. And I behaved like a bully, just like I learned from Dad.

Dad didn't treat me any differently for not being friends with . Gail.

It was almost the end of ninth grade when I apologized to Gail. I said I was sorry for how I had been acting. I said that I didn't have any reason for my behavior. She hadn't done anything wrong. I was just mean. Our friendship continued on like nothing had happened.

At home I heard from Dad. "Oh, so now you are friends again? Just like that? Friends? You watch yourself, young lady. Just watch yourself." Dad was always going to be Dad with his quirky mean behavior.

Years later, I connected my angry outburst with the beginning of normal teenage changes. My brain was beginning to rewire itself and not all my brain cells were connecting. In my teenage mind I was doing the right thing by "breaking up" with Gail. Well, that was my reasoning, anyway!

Chapter 17

Models from England were all the rage! They were fashionably skinny, with dark eyeliner and black false eyelashes. They would often wear mini-skirts, tight poorboy sweaters and white Go-Go boots. I wanted to wear black eyeliner and mascara to make my eyes dark like the models. I also wanted to wear a mini skirt but skip the tight sweater and Go-Go boots!

As you can imagine, a mini-skirt was ruled out by Dad. His rule was that when I knelt down the hem of my skirt or dress must touch the floor. Because I was tall, it seemed my skirts were longer then everyone else's. According to Mrs. Dreyfus, when she measured me to adjust a dress pattern to fit, she announced I had "disproportionately long thighs." This meant my skirts had to cover more leg then everyone else's. That's why my skirts seemed so long.

I rebelled against wearing long skirts by figuring out two ways to temporarily shorten my skirts. When I waited for the bus in the morning, I rolled my skirt waistband and shortened my skirt to whichever length I wanted. I unrolled the waistband before I got home after school. The second way I worked around my Dad's restrictions was to tape the hem up, which I usually did to shorten my dresses to the length I wanted. I removed the tape before I got home.

Then I had my methods of experimenting with makeup. I looked at the available makeup at our local drug store and realized I would be spending a lot of babysitting money for the makeup I wanted. Girls at school wore Cover Girl™ liquid foundation and powder, blush on their cheeks, thick black mascara, and black eyeliner that winged up at the outside edges of their eyes. Some even wore bright blue or turquoise eye shadow. I wanted to wear makeup like them.

My goal was to look like the fashion models in the magazines. I tried a friend's liquid eyeliner in black. Wet eyeliner smeared all over my eye area when I blinked. It took many tries to get my left eyeliner to match my right. Once it was on my eyelid I needed to keep my eye closed until it dried. I learned to make a thin black line that dried fast.

Then came the mascara. I asked my Great Auntie May about her mascara because she always had thick, butterfly-like, black eyelashes. She told me her secret was to coat her eyelashes with face powder before putting on the first coat of mascara. She would apply two or three coats each of powder then mascara. She taught me to be sure that each coat of mascara was completely dry before applying the next coat. I had to remember not to blink with wet mascara on my lashes. I looked like I had black butterflies above and below my eyes if I blinked when the mascara was wet.

At school the girls reapplied makeup after gym class and showers. I asked to try different shades of their foundation so I could figure out what color would look best on my skin. I found a color that looked perfect in the florescent lights of the girls' bathroom. However, when I went out in the sunlight, my face looked orange! Obviously there was more to choosing the right color foundation.

Great Auntie May helped me to pick the best color of liquid foundation and she bought me a cover-up stick to use over my blemishes. (Auntie May never said pimples, or acne, always blemishes.) At that time I still used Clearasil™ to cover my acne. I got better at blending the edges so the Clearasil was almost unnoticeable even in bright sunlight. It had been several years since Dad's comment about my blotchy skin and poor coverage with Clearasil.

After school I stopped at a friend's house to put on makeup before I went home. I wanted to show off my new fashion model look at home that night. My friend and her Mom helped me and I thought I finally looked great. Not exactly like a fashion model, but a fairly nice version of Sharmay.

As you can imagine, the "fashion model look" with makeup was *not* acceptable at home. However, I was not at all prepared for Dad's violent reaction.

"Only tramps wear makeup!" shouted Dad as he grabbed my chin and turned my face back and forth. Then he yanked me by my upper arm, pulled me down the hall and pushed me into the bathroom while he continued to shout, "Get that off your face, now! Wash it off!"

"Really? Auntie May is a tramp?" I couldn't help asking.

"Don't sass me girl! Look around, everywhere you go, tramps wear makeup. You don't see your mother with makeup on, do you?"

"No, but she could try some. It would brighten her cheeks and eyes like Auntie May's."

"I said 'Don't sass me' and I've had enough of you tonight young lady." Dad slapped me across my cheek. "There, that'll add some of that color you wanted on your face. Now get that stuff off. NOW!"

I was shocked at the slap, burst into tears, and slammed the bathroom door. You can imagine how awful I looked. Tears made the black eye makeup run down my face in streaks. I washed it all off. There was a red mark on my cheek where Dad hit me.

Did that stop me from wearing makeup? Nope! I put Clearasil on at home in the morning. When I got to school, I went directly to the gym bathroom and put on the rest of my makeup, foundation, blush, mascara and eyeliner. When I left school I washed it all off before going home.

That worked until the day that I didn't get all my makeup off and Dad noticed it at the dinner table. He grabbed my schoolbag and dumped it out on the kitchen counter. And one by one, he threw each item of makeup in the garbage. He informed me again that I was acting like a tramp, a disobedient tramp. "What is wrong with you? Don't you ever listen to me?"

I knew those were just rhetorical questions, like I learned in English class. I did not answer. I just glared and bit the insides of my cheeks to keep my mouth shut.

Dad shouted, "Get to your room!" He didn't hit me this time. I didn't mouth off and he didn't hit me, although I thought he was going to. Progress.

I was back to borrowing friends' makeup at school again. When I had enough babysitting money saved to buy my own makeup again, I didn't bring any home with me. I kept it safe in my gym locker at school along with my hairspray and perfume. Hairspray and perfume weren't allowed either.

Have you seen pictures of the sixties hairstyles? Big, poufy beehive hairdos were all the rage. Poufy French Twists looked classy. To get those hairstyles to stay in place, hairspray was used: lots and lots of hairspray. I wasn't allowed to use any because "tramps used hairspray." I wasn't a tramp. I was starting to catch on to some of Dad's quirks.

During ninth grade, Mom gave my hair a "permanent wave" and it looked awesome! It had nice flips on the ends and it "ratted" into a poof on top that I could clip a bow onto. I heard many comments like "What did you do to your hair? It looks great!" "Nice hairdo." "Did you set it with Dippity-Do™?" "How did you get your hair to flip up on the ends like that?" Soon other girls in school permed their hair but mine turned out the best!

My hair routine was extensive. First, I would wash my hair with a gentle, baby shampoo. Then I would comb a setting gel, like "Dippity-Do," through my hair. Next I would divide my hair into equal sections and roll it on big pink sponge rollers. Then I would sleep with these rollers in my hair to let it dry naturally overnight. I could also sit under a hairdryer until it was dry, but I still had to leave the curlers in overnight.

In the morning, I would unroll my hair and gently comb through it to not disturb the curls too much until I got to school. Then, in the gym locker room after putting on my makeup, I could do my hair. First I would "rat it" by spraying each ratted section with hair spray. Ratting was backcombing with a fine tooth comb or a brush. Aquanet™ hairspray was an inexpensive brand and it held hair nice and stiff. When all the hair was ratted, I could spray and shape it however I liked: Beehive, French Twist, a flip on the ends, or curling the ends under in a pageboy style. Every style was held in place with hairspray. Lots and lots of hairspray.

I liked having my hair in a flip or a pageboy. Poufy on top and either a little bow clipped near my bangs or a headband to hold my hair off my face. My hair style was shaped with Dippity-Do and Aquanet hairspray. I liked it!

Then one day, Dad saw me before I had combed my hair out flat and washed all my makeup off. "What is THAT supposed to be? A rat's nest? Only tramps do that to their hair. It's too old for you. Flatten it down. NOW!" Then he called on my mother. "Sharleen! Did you tell her she could wear her hair like this? Looking like a tramp?"

Mom replied, "I don't care what she does, as long as she graduates from high school. Will her hairstyle keep her from going to classes? Leave her be, David. You are only making the situation worse."

"Don't smart with me. Go fix her hair. I will not have her looking like a tramp." Turning to me he said, "And get that makeup off your face while your mother fixes your hair."

I ran to the bathroom. "I can do it myself. I'm not a baby you know."

"You sure could have fooled me, the way you act." Dad shouted after me.

"Just leave me alone!"

"What's Dad's big deal with tramps?" I asked Mom. She rolled her eyes and turned around to go back into the kitchen. I wonder if Dad secretly watched the "tramps." Otherwise, how did he know so much about them? Because I was crying, my black eye makeup ran from my eyes down my face. Again. I washed my face and got all my makeup off. Then I covered zits with Clearasil, as usual.

I tied a blue bandana over my hair like Lucille Ball did when she was cleaning on her I Love Lucy© TV show. Dad made me take off the bandana. Finally, my hair was flat enough for him. My hair was stuck flat against my head but I looked acceptable for my Dad.

Section Four

■ Lessons Learned

Chapter 18

I was alone downstairs in the basement playing bumper pool and listening to songs on my record player: "I am a rock, I am an island and a rock feels no pain and an island never cries©." What depressing song lyrics to be running over and over through my mind!

Another song I played repeatedly was the Zombies' 1968 song "It's the Time of the Season©." The first forty-five record I bought was "My Boyfriend's Back©" by the Angels. It was popular in 1963. I played those records over and over until I knew every word and every note.

I learned unwritten family rules of how to stifle feelings, no matter how hurtful or devastating. I learned how to show no pain and keep a stiff upper lip. I learned how not to air dirty laundry. I learned that my family cared about what the neighbors thought of them.

Why would I care what the neighbors thought? Apparently appearances were more important than my feelings. "I am a rock and a rock feels no pain." There you have it. The song loop that guided my teen feelings.

Dad came halfway down the basement stairs to see what I was doing. What? He didn't hear the records playing? "Get upstairs. Join the family," he curtly ordered.

"Nope."

"Don't sass me, girl!" He growled, "I don't want anyone to see or hear your behavior, especially your brother and sister. Now get upstairs and join the family."

Why must I join the family in the living room with the freaking TV on? Noise clutter. I did not bother anyone by playing bumper pool or the pinball machine. "Just leave me alone. My homework is done."

"Then go to your room." He stood on the stairs until I moved over to the record player.

"Fine." I turned off the record player and stood at the bottom of the stairs waiting for Dad to move out of my way. I didn't want to pass him on the stairs. Dad turned around and stomped back to the living room.

"Where's Sharmay?" Mom asked.

"In her room. She doesn't want to be a part of this family," Dad replied.

This scenario was repeated over and over on the weeknights Dad was home. Often, instead of going to the basement for music, bumper pool or pinball after dinner (5:30 sharp!) I went directly to my room. I chose no TV, but I also chose quiet. No brother and sister arguing. No hostile conversations or glaring looks between Mom and Dad.

I learned to be stoic, like a statue without feelings. I dealt by giving no responses, not communicating and not interacting with the family. Just a stoic statue.

No one showed me how to respect myself. If anyone tried to reach out to me, I resisted. I had an emotional barrier. Regardless of what events happened to me, I did not show emotion. No fear, no regret, no sadness, nothing. "And a rock feels no pain©."

Why talk when Dad would remind me, "Have your brain in gear before your mouth is in action"? If my brain was not in gear, and that was usually the case according to Dad, then he interrupted me by cutting off my sentence and shouting at me, "Do you remember me telling you to have your brain in gear before your mouth was in action? Do you? DO YOU?"

Of course, I nodded my head yes. "Well, then don't talk until your brain is in gear." So, I rarely talked. And I didn't feel any pain either. I stifled myself. "Don't talk, don't feel any pain, carry on!"

was my motto. I didn't know that family interactions could be any different.

Family responses weren't much better when something positive happened. For example, during junior high I represented our school in the long jump competition. I won the long jump many times at junior and senior high school meets and competed in the regional competitions.

When I came home from a track meet and announced I won first place in our sectional competition Mom replied, "Well, don't break your arm patting yourself on the back. Dinner's ready. Set the table." I didn't mention winning again. I was proud of winning and was not recognized for it at all.

I perceived myself as dumb. I couldn't figure anything out, and couldn't even use a key without bending it. If Mom or Dad said to do something "this way," I did it a different way. "I'll show them" was my attitude. Typical teen behavior. If there was a harder way to do something, that is what I chose. I unconsciously worked to sabotage myself. I didn't think situations through. I acted on impulse. I was driven to survive "my way and my way only." I was happy when I was alone.

"Just stay in your room, we don't want you ruining our family get together. You ruin every holiday and birthday with your obnoxious attitude." Dad, again, did not want me around.

"FINE!" I yelled as I slammed my bedroom door. I really must be defective, always wrong, bad and ugly looking.

"What are those spots on your face?" Freakin' Dad, he knew they were zits. He just wanted to humiliate me further.

"Stay out of sight in your room."

I thought, "Just try and get me to come out." I didn't say it out loud. My bedroom was my space. I stayed in my room where I felt safe and just a little bit happy.

"Why is Dad so mean to me?" I asked Mom one evening.

"He only wants what's best for you."

"Really? That's why he's mean? Calls me a tramp and pushes me around? That's what's best for me?"

"He doesn't want you to be wild like some of the neighbor's kids. Smoking behind their parents' backs. We see them smoking behind our garage out by the creek."

"That's being wild? Smoking would make me a tramp? Makeup, poufy hair, running and smoking would make me a tramp? I thought a tramp was like Freddy the Freeloader on the Red Skelton Show©.

You know a tramp is like a hobo? Auntie May wears makeup and high heels all the time! And her hair is poufy and she smokes, too!"

"Get a grip, Sharmay. You know what I mean. Don't go off on these tangents."

"I am trying to have a discussion. Just talking. Trying to figure this out. Dad's weird."

"That's ENOUGH!" Mom spun on her heels and walked away.

"Fine! I'm done here anyway. You don't care either!" I mumbled as I closed my bedroom door. I did not slam it, just closed it gently. I think Mom thought Dad was weird too and she couldn't face it. So when I said he was weird she ended our talk. This might have been the longest discussion Mom and I had for years. Years!

We were almost listening and responding to each other. Almost.

Chapter 19

I did not have any interest in joining Job's Daughters. My parents had already decided that I would join when I turned twelve. Mandatory participation. I knew the Job's Daughters was divided by Bethels throughout the worldwide organization. The Bethels were identified by numbers; I joined Bethel 53. My mother had belonged to Job's Daughters Bethel 5 when she was their Drill Team Captain.

Every other Saturday afternoon I was dropped off in the Masonic Lodge parking lot where Bethel 53 held their meetings. Parents were a big support for their daughters during the meetings and at other Job's Daughters events. I attended meetings and events alone.

Mom did provide a lot of cardboard for the Job's Daughters fundraiser newspaper drives. She cut up the heavy corrugated cardboard flower boxes from Grandma Lucille's flower store. Mom saved the boxes in our garage and cut them into manageable size pieces then tied them into bundles. We usually had several station wagons full to deliver for the newspaper drive. This recycled cardboard earned more money than all the newspapers that were collected by the other members.

Job's Daughters offered several activities besides the twice-monthly official meetings. Every spring I played on their softball team. September through February the drill team practiced on Monday nights for two hours in preparation for the annual state wide competition held every February at the Milwaukee Auditorium.

Our Bethel 53 Job's Daughters drill team went to the National Drill Team Competition in Philadelphia, Pennsylvania during the summer of 1966. On the bus the book "The Group" by Mary McCarthy was passed around. Several of the older high school girls made sure everyone completed their "required" reading of the "sex education stories," whether we wanted to read it or not.

I learned about the mechanics of sex from several scenes in The Group©. Sex is what? That goes in where? It's supposed to do what? Most of all, why would anyone do "that" if the outcome could be pregnancy? If you were pregnant, then everyone knew what you did. I just didn't get it. I flunked my first sex education. I never figured out why this book did not get confiscated by the parents that chaperoned on the trip.

By the time I was in high school I learned from Job's Daughters that when you had a boyfriend, you had sex. Then you might run away with your boyfriend and get married because you were pregnant. Or run away and give your baby up for adoption. Or have a quick wedding and stop going to school. It seemed odd that my parents wanted me to learn these behaviors from the "good girls" at Job's Daughters.

Believe me when I say I learned important life lessons from the older Job's Daughters girls' behaviors. It was an effective life lesson for a teenage girl to experience the outcomes from girls dropping out of high school to have a baby and/or give their baby up for adoption or get married. Either way, the girl was not allowed to attend our high school once she became pregnant. She could not even return after the baby was born. To tell a young girl how not to behave because of possible outcomes was not the same as experiencing a Job's Daughters member facing choices due to pregnancy.

Here was my goal for high school: do not get pregnant. Do not behave in any way that could prevent me from graduating from high school. Just graduate from high school!

(By the way, Mom was a Job's Daughter when she and my Dad created me!)

Chapter 20

Near the end of eighth grade, I read a pamphlet on a school bulletin board and found out that the Milwaukee Public School System offered non-credit summer school classes. The six- week classes were free and offered at local high schools. I went to the school office and signed up for Speed Reading and Note Taking, which were available at Custer High School, our local high school.

I should have asked my parents before I signed up. They were not happy that I decided to go to summer school without asking for permission. Apparently, my plan to be in summer school for six weeks was going to change Mom's summer work plans.

Mom said, "There you go again, thinking of yourself and not how your actions affect everyone in our family." I caused this family issue by planning to do something for myself.

I completed the summer school classes and really enjoyed myself. I was at the high school like an older teenager, not like an almost fourteen-year-old. And oh, the boys! These were young men with driver's licenses. I was just a ninth grader and not even going to the high school in fall. I had one more year in junior high. Sigh. The high school boys still were cute!

Shortly after summer school ended, I received a surprise in the mail. It was my summer school transcript, which showed that I had earned one high school credit that summer. I earned half a credit for Speed Reading and another half credit for Note Taking. I did not expect to earn high school credit for these courses. The pamphlet said the courses were non-credit if the student was not currently enrolled in high school.

I was not currently enrolled in high school, but I was already earning high school credits. Due to the SAP program, I took ninth grade English, Math and Science during eighth grade and earned three credits. I now had earned four high school credits before I started ninth grade! Wow!

A plan had started to rumble in the back of my mind that maybe I could graduate from high school early. I knew I would earn three more credits for the tenth grade English, Math and Science classes I was taking during ninth grade. If I went to Summer School after ninth grade then I could start high school with at least eight credits earned before I started tenth grade.

Let me explain about earning high school credits early. Because I was in the SAP program, during seventh grade I completed both seventh and eighth grade Math, English and Science. In eighth grade I completed ninth grade Math, English and Science, which were high school level courses. I earned three credits towards high school graduation while only in eighth grade. In ninth grade I took tenth grade Math, English and Science courses and earned another three credits.

I completed Summer School after both eighth and ninth grade earning one credit each summer. I had eight credits before I started high school which turned out to be a life changing accomplishment. I realized I could graduate high school at least one year early. My goal was set. I would accomplish it!

I could earn the credits, but would Mom and Dad agree to let me graduate early? I needed parental permission to graduate because I was under 18 years old. What kind of school system was that? I could earn the required credits to graduate but be denied graduation because my parents might not give me permission to graduate. That was a scary thought. Somehow I needed to get along with my parents, if only to receive their permission to graduate high school early. I think they wanted me out of the house as soon as possible too, so graduating early would help their cause.

I began volunteer work the summer after ninth grade. Volunteers had to be at least fourteen years old at the Jewish Home for the Aged. I started as a volunteer the Tuesday after I turned fourteen, July 1967. Most Tuesday afternoons I volunteered for two to four hours. I was usually in the Occupational Therapy (OT) department coordinating projects for the residents to complete. I set up the type setting for the printed dinner invitations, dinner napkins, or thank-you notes the home sold. Sometimes I went to the residents' rooms and scheduled time for them to complete OT projects.

I earned an award for the number of volunteer hours I put in during my first year. I looked forward to when I would be sixteen. Then I could volunteer as a Candy Striper, and be able to wear a uniform. As a Candy Striper I would be allowed to go into patient rooms to make deliveries, refill ice buckets or other non-nurse type work.

I wasn't working at the family flower store and earning money on the days I volunteered at the Jewish Home for the Aged. Grandma Lucille paid me anyway, as if I was working, so I didn't lose any income. Being paid by Grandma Lucille was a secret.

Often during my teen years Grandma Lucille talked with me about working in the nursing field. She said things like, "No one can take your education away from you and nursing is a job you can do anywhere. You can always do some other type of work, if you want, after you earn your nursing degree. And you would always have nursing to go back to at anytime."

Did I want to be a nurse? Not specifically, but I learned that I liked to work with people. Office work was boring at the Jewish Home and I didn't feel like I accomplished anything worthwhile doing office tasks. Honestly, I liked working directly with people. Nursing as a career was something for me to think about for the future.

Like I ever would have a future.

Chapter 21

Hiding in my room, I called the flower store using the princess phone I took out of Mom and Dad's bedroom. Auntie May answered, then said, "Lucille, pick up. Sharmay's in tears."

"I can't come to the store today," I sobbed to my Grandmother. "I've been grounded for sassing Mom. Dad won't let me leave the house." The flower store was my job. I earned money when I worked there. "He's not being fair."

"Don't worry about your job. It'll be here for you. It's just 'growing pains.' We have all been through it and it'll get better," my Grandma Lucille soothed me.

"When? Will I live long enough?" I heard about "teenage angst & growing pains" when I talked with Grandma Lucille.

"Of course you will live through this. You could change schools. Go to the Lutheran High down the road from me."

"Dad won't let me go to school there; so he can keep control of me."

"Is that how it feels? I know he's rough on you. He just wants the best for you."

"So he's mean to me for my own good? Like that's supposed to help me?"

"He doesn't know any other way. It's how he grew up," Grandma Lucille tried to give me some context.

"So why torture me? I'm not him. I can't stand it anymore!" I yelped. "I just want to run away or die or something to get this over with."

"I know it seems hard right now. Just keep doin' your best and it'll all work out. Talk to your Guardian Angels about it. They'll help you."

"Maybe. Hopefully I can get to the store tomorrow." Dad opened my bedroom door without knocking. "I gotta go. Bye."

I wondered if he had been standing outside my bedroom door listening to me on the phone. Of course he knew I was on the phone. The telephone cord was on the floor and came out of his bedroom and into mine. He heard me talking for sure!

"Who were you on the phone with? Why are you using my phone in here?" he demanded.

"Grandma Lucille. Where else am I supposed to talk with her? In the kitchen so everyone can hear?"

"This is my phone. You ask to use it. Do not go in my room and take the phone. And leave your door open."

"Fine." I picked up a book and started reading.

"Did you hear me?" my Dad asked.

"I said 'fine.' I'm busy." I looked down at my book thinking leave me alone, just leave me alone. Just go away. Dad picked up his princess phone and took it back into his bedroom. I reached up and slammed my bedroom door.

Dad immediately threw the door open. "I said, 'Leave your door open,' and I meant it! You're on thin ice here. Don't push me!"

I looked up and repeated "FINE!" while I continued to read. I mumbled, "Just leave me alone."

"Ok, Toots, that didn't go so well for someone who wants to try to get along with her parents." I heard this voice in my left ear.

Who was talking in my ear? I was alone! I heard the voice again. *"I'm the Guardian Angel your Grandma talked about!"*

Weird, that's for sure.

Later that week, I was at the flower store talking with Mom, Auntie May, Grandma Lucille, and Grandpa Al.

"What's up with Dad and his obsession with 'tramps'? Everyone wears makeup and rats their hair. It's the style now. It doesn't mean

I'm a tramp, one of the floozy type women. He's so old-fashioned. I just wanna look good and be like everyone else".

"He had bad mentors growing up," Mom finally shared. "His dad went to bars, gambled and paid attention to the 'ladies.' They lost their house before Grandma Prestin divorced him."

"So he thinks I'm a tramp? Like I've inherited some bad traits from his father; a man I have never met, by the way? Dad assumes I'm bad. I just want to be like everyone else around school. It's not fair. He's mean to me. Really mean to me, and I haven't done anything to be treated like that. I like it better when he's gone to his meetings. Then he isn't around to make me feel ugly and stupid.

"He throws away my homework because he thinks it isn't good enough. What does he know about it? It's so humiliating." I couldn't even mention how bad I felt about myself when he pointed out my pimples. I couldn't talk about that. "He pokes fun at me and I get so mad at him. It's like he wants me to feel bad and get mad so he can be superior because he is the know-it-all Dad."

My rant continued. "Then he sends me to my room so he doesn't have to put up with me. He can just be with his 'real family.' I'm just the trouble maker. WHY? I'm not bad. I try to get good grades and have friends. But my friends don't meet his requirements. So I don't invite Gail, or anyone else to our house. Even the neighborhood girls don't want to come over because of him. He's not nice. Well, it's not my fault! I didn't do anything to be treated like this. I'm just trying to grow up and be normal and have a normal life.

"He pokes fun at me and tries to make me get mad so he can yell at me. Then he acts like he is the better person and I'm the wacky kid who goes off her rocker. He is so against everything I want to do. My friends aren't good enough. I don't trust him. He looks through my stuff and listens on the phone extension. It's like he's trying to trap me into doing something wrong. Then he says he can do that because I live in his house. Like he's king, or something. He's a weirdo, a freakin' weirdo, and he's trying to drive me crazy so he can kick me out of the house and justify it."

That was the most I've ever said in my life about anything. Ever. And no one interrupted me or told me to stop talking or anything. Mom gave me a few of her "you're so exasperating" type of looks but still, no one interrupted me. I think they were all speechless with the issues I was spewing out.

Section Five

■ Lessons Learned

Chapter 22

One cold winter afternoon in tenth grade, I skipped gym class. I walked to a diner that was several blocks from school. After eating a cheeseburger and drinking a root beer float, I walked back towards school, and in the school parking lot I ran into Robert and Paul.

Robert was a friend's older brother and Paul I knew by sight. Neither were in any of my classes. They were going to McGovern Park in Paul's 1960 four door Chevy. McGovern Park was a favorite hangout of high school kids. I decided to go along for the ride because they assured me I would get back to school in time for my next class.

"*Toots, Toots stay at school.*" There was my Guardian Angel in my left ear again. Was I schizophrenic? Hearing voices?

I rode in the back seat (alone!) on the drive to the park. We all got out of the car and sat on picnic tables talking. Shortly after we arrived the police came through the park. I was taken to the local police station and my parents were called to pick me up. I had to wait at the police station until after dinner when Dad was available to pick me up. I remember the date being December 13 because my Mom accused me of trying to ruin her birthday, which was December 14.

I was humiliated. I stopped all thoughts and I tried to send my mind somewhere else. Then I remembered the voice that popped into my left ear. My Guardian Angel was offering me guidance, a warning, really.

I knew I couldn't tell anyone about the left ear voice or they would think I was wacky for sure. I just wanted to be out of the police station which smelled of oil paint. Most of the building was painted a "soothing" pea green color. I wanted to be at home listening to records in the basement. "I am a rock and a rock feels no pain."

It got a bit worse than just getting caught skipping school. Not only did I skip school and get caught, I was alone in a car with two teenage boys. Paul had beer in the trunk of his car and he was cited with some violation for having alcohol in the presence of a minor. That was me, the minor. I pleaded with Mom and Dad to get the charges against Paul dropped. No one had been drinking beer that afternoon.

Several weeks later, my parents and I went to court in Paul's defense and the charges against him were dismissed. It was not a very fun day off. My parents pointed out to me that they both had to take the day off work and did not earn any money because they had to go to court. My behavior caused a loss of family income. Well, it was my fault for skipping school so you'd think I'd learned my lesson.

Apparently not.

I continued to skip gym class and go off school campus but I never again rode in anyone's car when I skipped school. I walked wherever I went! Lesson learned. Oh, wait, I still skipped class and left campus. *Almost* lesson learned.

When Gail's brother, Chuck, heard about my McGovern Park/ police station adventure he was not a happy guy. "We need to talk."

"Sure."

"No, really, we need to talk," Chuck insisted. "I know those guys. You don't want to be hanging around them. When can we talk? Soon, Sharmay, I mean it. We need to talk soon."

"Like when?" I went to work at the flower store directly from school and Chuck worked delivering pizzas in the evenings.

"I'll call you."

"NO!" I exclaimed. "No one can know we talk. Especially not my parents." Remember, Chuck was both a boy and from the "wrong side of the tracks." And he was Gail's brother which made our friendship an awkward situation. Dad would say, "You know what he's really after, don't you? DON'T YOU?" I thought of a reply like, "Maybe that's how you were as a teenager and that's why you're so weird about my friends now." Dad would probably knock me senseless if I said any of that to him. But I sure thought about saying it.

"I'll stop over at your house."

"That would be worse! We'll talk somewhere around school. Something will work out." He had a car. We could talk in his car as long as no one saw us together. Again in a car with a teenaged boy, older than me. That could really be trouble if Dad found out. It was pathetic that I needed to sneak around to talk with my friends. I couldn't even invite them over to the house like normal people did. My parents' behavior encouraged me to have covert friendships. I hid my friends because they didn't meet my parents' criteria as perfect people.

A dentist appointment soon provided a perfect opportunity to talk with Chuck. Instead of taking a city bus to the dentist's office, Chuck would pick me up at school and drive me to the dentist.

We talked on the way. He was kind and concerned that I might be hanging around with guys who could get me "in trouble." Like being taken to the police station wasn't already in trouble? I also knew about "getting in trouble" from Job's Daughters. "Don't be worried about me," I told him.

Chuck also wanted to smooth over problems with me trying to talk with my parents. He offered me some advice. Sort of a summary of tips on "How to talk to parents of teenagers" and at the same time, "What not to say or do that might make your parents more angry."

Really, there was no way to talk with my parents about anything. They made rules. I had to follow them. I could not challenge their rules. I was not 18 and I was living under their roof. Until I moved out, I had to follow the rules and shut up about it. I had to be an example for my sister and brother. "Don't cause problems. Get it?"

Yeah, I got it. No discussing anything. It was their way or no way. I had to keep my mouth shut about everything, always.

Chuck said, "Don't make it any harder on yourself then it already is. We all agree there is some big resentment brewing with your Dad. It's like he's out to get you. He lurks around ready to catch you not following his rules."

"Thanks for trying. I hope I live through all this. Thanks for driving me home today. Gotta go."

While I was sitting in the dentist's chair the left ear voice said, "*Toots, listen to Chuck. Really listen to him. He's trying to help.*" What was up with this left ear voice? It was scary. I may have needed more help than Chuck could offer.

Several weeks later, Chuck enlisted in the Army and was gone. Just like that, he was gone. I no longer had a borrowed older brother to offer me support and common sense. Whether I wanted his advice or not, I got it.

When Chuck came home after basic training there wasn't any time to catch up on stuff going on around high school. Until he came home on leave, I didn't realize that I missed talking with him. No one else talked to me about day-to-day common sense stuff like he did. I couldn't tell anyone how I felt, not even his sister. I learned to keep everything I felt as a secret.

Chuck helped me understand a lot about teenage behavior, parents' perceptions and how to get through it all without alienating my family. Good thing he intervened! I imagine how rebellious I could have been without his input. I treated Chuck poorly, really, I disrespected him.

Several times during our sophomore year in high school, my friend Cheryl's Dad drove Cheryl and me to a teenage dance held once a month on a Friday night in Mequon in the gymnasium of a Catholic School. The dance was sponsored by the Catholic Churches in the area and was chaperoned by parents from different churches.

Sometimes Cheryl's parents chaperoned. I called them Mom Q and Dad Q.

The Mequon dance was where I met John. I saw him there several times. I never saw him dance or hang out with any girls at the dance. One night I saw him leaving the dance and he drove away in a dusty rose-colored four door 1968 Oldsmobile that looked to be in really good condition. This car was like the one my Grandpa Wally might drive. Another night I saw John bring several girls to the dance. It turned out he drove his sister and her friends to the dance. Sometimes he would stay and listen to the band.

The first night I talked with him he was standing along the wall with his friend Ryan. Ryan was interested in dancing with my friend Cheryl, but was too shy to ask her. Both John and Ryan walked over to where Cheryl and I stood along a wall. Cheryl and Ryan went onto the dance floor. I was stuck talking to this tall, blonde guy named John. I found out he drove the nice Oldsmobile because his father was a car salesman and his dad often drove the sale cars. John liked the Olds so his dad let him drive it on weekends.

According to John, "The dance was for teeny-boppers." Unless he liked the band that was playing, he didn't come into the dance. After the dance, cars would line up on the driveway in front of the building, waiting to pick up the kids who attended the dance. If

John did not attend the dance then he would be in the car lineup waiting to pick up his sister and friends. I started looking for him at the monthly dance.

One day when I was leaving school, I saw the Oldsmobile in the high school parking lot. John was there picking up his sister. I really didn't like John but I liked the idea of John. Older guy, drove a nice car, picked his sister up from school and took her and her friends to the Catholic school dances. Something about him offered me comfort when I talked with him. He was "different" in a way that was different from how my family had our dysfunctional interactions. Maybe his "different" way was closer to normal.

Chapter 23

Cheryl got her driver's license in the spring of tenth grade and she was allowed to drive her Dad's 1963 Buick Skylark to school. Only driving to and from school was allowed. Her Dad kept track of Cheryl's exact mileage. He also always, *always* knew exactly how much gas was in his car. Gas was 19 cents a gallon at that time!

Cheryl and I wanted to drive around during our lunch hour. We solved the mileage issue by disconnecting the speedometer cable. If the speedometer cable was not connected then no mileage was recorded. We would guess at the number by putting the correct amount of gas to get the gas gauge back up to the correct level. Most times it was only 10 cents. How were we to know that the gas station attendant was a friend of her Dad?

We thought we were getting away with something driving around at lunch in Dad Q's car. We usually went to the local diner for a burger, fries and root beer. We acted like cool teenagers with a car to drive. That is, until the day the speedometer cable broke when as we reconnected it.

Cheryl and I could not think of any story to explain how the cable broke so we decided to tell the truth. Both of us were very nervous on the drive home to Cheryl's house. We rehearsed our short speech.

We walked into her house. Dad Q was sitting on the couch watching TV drinking a beer. At the same time Cheryl and I said, "Can you come outside? We need to tell you something about your car."

He looked at us and asked, "Is it smashed up?"

"No!"

"Then it can't be too bad." He stood up and laughed, "What did you two do now?" As we struggled to tell him the problem, we walked to his car. Cheryl opened the car door and showed him the cable hanging under the steering wheel.

"It was bound to happen," her Dad laughed. "You can't keep disconnecting and reconnecting it. Eventually the connector breaks off." Dad Q walked into their garage and came back out and handed Cheryl a new speedometer cable. "Did you really think I didn't know what you two were doing? I have eyes in the back of my head, you know! Now you both can figure out how to replace it!" He returned to the house. A few minutes later he came back outside and helped us replace the cable. He wanted to be sure we didn't mess up and wreck the car. "I want it done right," Dad Q said. We also had to change the oil in the car for him that day.

Dad Q did not say any nasty words or demeaning comments. Cheryl wasn't grounded and continued to drive his car to school. If we took it somewhere during lunch break the car needed to be returned with a full tank of gas. We didn't drive around as often during lunch break after the speedometer cable was replaced. Maybe because we weren't breaking any rules anymore and the excitement factor was gone. We had permission to drive the car at lunch. Returning the car with a full gas tank wasn't a problem either.

I could not even imagine how horrible the situation would have been if I needed to tell my Dad about breaking the speedometer cable on his car. It would not have been a laughing matter, that's for sure. I liked being at Cheryl's house and with her family.

I spent more and more time with Cheryl and her family. Several times during the summer I went camping with her family on the weekends. Cheryl and I slept in the back of their station wagon because there wasn't enough room in their camper for both Cheryl and me. During this time, I learned about loving, caring family members who enjoyed being with each other and treated one another with respect.

During the spring of tenth grade, when I was fifteen years and nine months old, I was allowed to take Driver's Education class. This included "real" driving after school. During one class, one student driver was at the wheel while another student driver and I were in the back seat waiting our turns to drive. Our instructor intended for us to practice parallel and angle parking that day and directed our current student driver to a parking lot in McGovern Park. This was the same park that I was at with Robert and Paul.

This time at the park I saw my friend, Phil, parked with his girlfriend in one of the parking lots. They were making out! I didn't know Phil was that kind of a guy! I knew Phil from our church.

Our instructor laughed and asked me to angle park next to Phil's car. I was told to get in the driver's seat. I was so embarrassed and nervous. I got into the driver's seat, completed all the pre-drive checks and for my first time ever, I backed out of an angled parking place. Both Phil and his girlfriend watched me closely as I backed out.

Success, I didn't hit Phil's car!

The driving challenges continued. I was told to parallel park between two cars on the street still in view of Phil's car. Of course

Phil and his girl continue to watch. Happily, I parallel parked the car on my first try. I loved the power steering because it made turning the wheel to park so easy. Then I was told to drive around the block and parallel park between the same two cars again. After the second time I parallel parked without a glitch, I was told to back the car into the parking lot and park next to Phil's car.

Back the car into a parking lot? Surprisingly, I backed up just fine! The third student driver got behind the driver's wheel. I collapsed in the back seat of the car both exhausted and proud of myself for parallel parking twice without any problems.

On my sixteenth birthday I passed my driver's test on my first try. Later that day I asked if I could drive Dad's stick shift car. He took me out for a short demo on how to drive with stick shift. This instruction lasted the length of two city blocks. "I've got it Dad. I can practice alone," I insisted. Despite Dad's protests, I drove him back to the house. "Out of the car, Dad. I can do this!" I declared triumphantly as I drove off to practice using a clutch and shifting.

I returned home in less than thirty minutes having mastered driving with stick shift. I got that shifting down fast! I wondered why my mother didn't drive stick shift. It occurred to me that if Mom drove stick then she would need to share a car with Dad. By not being able to drive stick she had her own car with an automatic transmission. I realized there was a method to Mom's choices.

It turned out when I returned home no one really cared that I passed my driver's test or that I just learned to drive stick shift. Everyone was sitting in front of the TV watching replays of the moon landing. Everyone watched as Neil Armstrong took his "one small step for man and one giant leap for mankind" and they were mesmerized to see the moon landing on TV.

I had my own small step that day but no one noticed. I went to my room.

Chapter 24

There was a time during high school when other students began to drink alcohol whenever it was accessible to them. Beer never appealed to me because of the yeasty smell and awful taste. Dad built a bar area in our basement and it was stocked with various types of liquor. He did not drink any alcohol. The liquor was at our house for his friends.

If the liquor bottle was open then I tried the liquor – straight. Everything I tried tasted horrible. Brandy, Gin, Vodka, Peppermint Schnapps, Whiskey and Scotch. I tried all of them. The Peppermint Schnapps was not too bad. It never occurred to me to mix the liquor with soda or water.

I bragged to friends about trying all the liquors and they wanted to try them too. So I figured out a way to take liquor to school in my purse. I used a plastic Phisohex™ soap bottle and filled it up with booze. It only held two ounces. The bottle was a solid green so no one could tell that it didn't have Phisohex in it.

In the girl's bathroom at school, where I would normally go to wash my face, put on makeup and style my hair, my friends and I would stand at the sinks and try the booze. Each day we had a different kind of booze to try. If one of my friends had access to liquor at home, or where they babysat, they would take the bottle and fill it up. There were 5 of us hiding out in the bathroom drinking booze. It was only about 2 swallows each but that was enough to get drunk; straight chugs of liquor.

Blackberry brandy was my downfall. I liked the blackberry brandy and I drank more than my fair share. Then I went to English class. I sat at my desk and got woozy. I had to lay my head on the desk which, of course, got the teacher's attention. I was sent to the Nurse's Office. Our School Nurse called my Mom at work to come pick me up.

I passed out while waiting for Mom and felt a little better by the time she got there.

"When did you get sick? You were fine this morning," Mom wondered.

"It came on real sudden. I got dizzy and felt like I was going to throw up. So I put my head on the desk. That's when I was sent to the Nurse's Office."

"Well, you lay down when we get home. Maybe you'll feel better by supper time."

Sure enough, we got home and I slept off the booze. I felt fine by 5:30 when supper was ready. When Dad got home he went through my purse and schoolbag. I was sure he was looking for evidence of why I was "sick." He never suspected the Phisohex bottle and didn't open it when he picked it up out of my purse. It was several weeks before he noticed there was less liquor in all his bottles. I denied knowing anything about it. I wouldn't confess to drinking his liquor.

That was the end of my drinking experiences. I never wanted to feel that sick again. I avoided taking any chugs from the Phisohex bottle when friends passed it around. I tipped the bottle and pretended to drink but never did again. Lesson learned! This lesson I learned well.

I did not have a "steady" boyfriend during high school. However, that John guy kept hanging around during eleventh grade, even though I was often rude to him. John enlisted in the Air Force. I went to Homecoming with someone else but John sent a dozen roses to the house the day of Homecoming.

I went to the February Job's Daughters Ball with Chuck but left with John. I went to the May Prom with John but left with Chuck. I don't remember the reason I left with Chuck or why I left the Job's

Daughters Ball with John. John would wear his Air Force Dress Uniform and Chuck would wear his Army Dress Uniform. Both boys were blonde and polite. If one wasn't around, the other was. Maybe I didn't have a steady "boyfriend," but I did have two friends who were older boys.

I was not allowed to have friends who happened to be boys, according to my Dad. Both Chuck and John *were* my friends. I had classmates who were boys and I considered them to be friends, too. I wondered why Dad didn't send me to an all girls school. Then I realized that all girls schools were private and he would have had to pay tuition for me. Dad was not going to pay for anything for me unless he was required to pay by law or something. According to Dad, I was nothing but trouble, even before I was born.

Chapter 25

During my last semester in high school I was caught leaving the school campus by Dad. This time I was in Cheryl's Dad's car. Cheryl was driving, I rode shotgun. She needed to get something at the local dime store several blocks from school.

Instead of turning left out of the school parking lot and going directly to the dime store Cheryl turned right, which took us onto the street in front of school. Dumb and double dumb! As we waited for traffic to clear to turn onto Villard Avenue to go north, my Dad was making a turn onto Villard Avenue to go south. He passed directly in front of us in his work van. Cheryl and I both waved like we were happy to see him. What else could we have done?

Before we drove out of the school parking lot I heard one of those weird left ear voice warnings. *"Toots, do not leave the school grounds."* Was that a direct order? Was it a premonition, déjà vu, a flash of things to come, a warning? Whatever you want to call it, like usual when I heard or felt those warnings, I ignored it and charged ahead without thinking of the consequences.

Could my Guardian Angel have been more direct? Every time I heard that voice in my left ear I resisted the common sense it offered. I ignored the information that would have helped me avoid getting into trouble.

Dad made a U-turn and followed us to the dime store's parking lot. He got out of his vehicle, stomped over to the car and yanked open the car door where I sat. "Get out of the car - NOW! Why aren't you in school?" He grabbed my right upper arm and yanked me out of the car, then pushed me towards the back door of his car and into the back seat while yelling, "Get in the car! NOW! GET IN THE CAR!"

While being pulled and pushed to his car I tried to explain why I was off school campus with Cheryl. "Well, Cheryl needed....."

"Cheryl needed? Why are you here? When you should be in school?" My Dad was furious.

"Well, I thought...."

"There you go - trying to think again! You are going right back to school where you belong."

As if I had any choice in the matter. He drove me directly back to school. Then he escorted me to the Principal's office where he reported me for skipping school. I received an immediate three-day suspension. Dad signed a form which had me immediately reinstated without the three days off. The purpose was to get "my bad behavior documented on my school records."

Due to the suspension, I was no longer eligible for any scholarships or grants that I had applied for to cover college tuition. Gee, thanks Dad.

Mom wrote all excused absence notes that went to the school office. These notes excused me from missing class due to illness, dentist appointments or other legitimate reasons to not be at school. I rewrote every note before turning it into the high school office. Every note in my record was in my hand writing, not Mom's. This included all the notes that excused me for the days I skipped gym class. That was until the day that Dad had me suspended and he saw the notes in my file. I don't remember what he yelled when he realized none of my absence excuses were in Mom's handwriting. I was caught for forging my excuses.

Whoopee ding fizz. I didn't care. What was the school going to do? Suspend me and put a "blot" on my record? Dad had already done that, thank you very much. I remember thinking, "Note to self – your purpose at school is to graduate. Keep your mouth shut! Do not argue with Dad." I did not argue. I kept "a stiff upper lip."

I knew more about that left ear voice before I left the school grounds. It was intuition, a warning, directly from my Guardian Angel to not skip school. If only I had learned to listen to the voice before the consequences.

"Well, what do you have to say for yourself now, young lady?" Dad asked while he kept his teeth clamped together.

"I'm waiting for my brain to get in gear before my mouth is in action."

"DO NOT SASS ME GIRL."

"Like I said, I'm waiting for my brain to get in gear," I insisted, throwing Dad's oft-repeated words back at him.

Dad grabbed my upper right arm and yanked me out of the high school office into the hallway. "Get back to your classes. I will deal with you at home tonight."

I went directly home after school and confessed to Mom about going to the dime store with Cheryl and Dad seeing us. I told her about being suspended and immediately reinstated. I did not tell her about her letters being rewritten by me. I don't think she ever found out.

When Dad got home from work he was quiet, really quiet. Then Dad said to Mom, "I'm done with Sharmay. I'm washing my hands of her. I'm done with her. I'm leaving her up to you now."

Moms reply was surprisingly blasé. "It's about time! I just want her to graduate."

I wasn't grounded or anything. They didn't even take away my telephone privileges. Dad just took away his parental responsibilities.

Chapter 26

During my sophomore and junior years in high school I completed extra classes which allowed me to earn more credits towards graduation. I was able to take these classes by giving up Study Halls. There was a minimum grade point average (GPA) requirement to give up Study Hall. I never lost the privilege to take extra classes. The high school credits added up quickly.

During a discussion with a high school guidance counselor in the fall of 1969 I learned that I had earned enough credits to graduate in January 1970. I did it! I was able to graduate early, yet I decided not to graduate in January. I would wait until June.

The second semester of my junior year, which became my senior year, I took Advanced Math, Physics and an English Literature class, which were only open to senior students. English Lit was boring to me. I also took Public Speaking and Advanced Note Taking. Both were helpful classes but not necessary for graduation.

I was concerned that my parents would not authorize my early graduation for my own good, or to teach me a lesson in who was boss of my life. I heard those words several times during arguments. To my great relief, my parents signed the permission slip that allowed me to graduate in June 1970, one year early. I would be graduating. That's what really mattered to all of us.

Not only were my grades often mixed up with the other Preston in my classes, the final mix-up was in the Custer High School 1970 Yearbook. Our names were mixed up beneath our senior pictures. How could our names have been reversed? I certainly looked like a girl in my picture and he looked like a boy in his. Maybe it was a final prank played on us by the seniors who were not happy that we both were graduating one year early.

Chapter 27

The spring prior to high school graduation, I started looking into nursing programs in the Milwaukee area. To keep my expenses down I wanted to continue to live at home, at my parents' house. After all the strife I planned to keep living at home.

Milwaukee Area Technical College (MATC) accepted me into their Associate Degree Nursing Program. The program was two years of eighteen credits each semester and one summer session of six credits. Two years of college and I would have an Associate Degree in Nursing (ADN). Then I could write the Wisconsin Registered Nurse Boards. If I wanted to, I could continue on with classes to earn my Bachelor of Science Degree in Nursing (BSN).

At home, there never was any discussion about me attending college. Shortly before graduation I informed my parents that I was accepted at MATC in their ADN program and intended to work as a RN after graduation. I did not receive support from Mom and Dad. I heard comments such as, "You think you can take care of sick people? Save their lives? Show up for shift work on weekends and holidays? Who are you trying to kid?"

"What? You don't believe in me?" I burst into tears. With those words I realized no matter what I did, or what field I studied in college, I would never be accepted by them. I was their "failure." I was graduating in the top third of my class and still my parents did not believe in me. I did not have their support or love. I continued to be a nobody in their eyes.

"We didn't plan for college. It's your education, you pay for it." Dad told me.

My parents didn't plan for me to go to college? What an insult.

To help me out, I was given my life insurance policy with a face value of two thousand five hundred dollars. It had a quarterly premium due the next month. I now had my first "adult" living expense handed to me "for my own good."

"If you need money that bad there is a cash value on this policy. Check it out. You might be able to borrow money from the policy, but you'll have to pay the quarterly premiums from now on."

"Thanks, Dad," I said glibly.

"Hey, I could have kept it for myself and cashed it in. After all, I've paid every penny of the premiums."

Now I had to find out what a life insurance policy was and how much the quarterly premiums were.

Chapter 28

My high school graduation was scheduled for June 1970. Then I found out that Dad did not plan to attend my graduation ceremony. He was going to be busy with a Masonic meeting the night of graduation.

Even after all of his rejection, I took this personally. Nothing I did was ever good enough for him. He wasn't even going to attend my graduation.

Before I knew this, I asked Dad, "I'm getting a ticket for you, right?"

"Why are you asking me?"

"I need to order tickets today."

"It's a Tuesday night. I have Masonic meetings on Tuesday nights. You know that."

In desperation for his approval, I begged. "Could you skip your meeting that week? Please? I only graduate from high school once."

"I told YOU I have a meeting!" Now Dad was getting angry.

"Skip it. Isn't my graduation more important than your meeting? Aren't I more important than your meeting?"

"I have a meeting! That is where I will be. At my meeting." Dad meant what he said when he declared he would wash his hands of me.

"That's not what I asked. Me, my high school graduation, or your meeting? Which is more important to you?"

Dad refused to answer. "Do NOT argue with me. I'm tired of your sassy mouth and belligerent attitude. Get out of my way. Go! Get out of my way NOW."

"David, what's going on?" Mom asked as she walked in through the back door. "I can hear you both yelling out in the garage."

"Stay out of this," my Dad dictated.

"He said he's got a meeting on Tuesday and won't be at graduation," I tattled.

"Sharleen, I said, stay out of this! Now get...."

"Get him a ticket. Just get him a ticket." Mom told me.

"I don't matter to you at all. Do I, Dad? Not at all! Your meeting is more important than seeing me, your DAUGHTER get her diploma and graduate. Enjoy your IMPORTANT meeting." I stared at him in contempt before shaking my head and walking away, trying not to let out an uncontrollable sob. I pulled my shoulders back, held my head high and thought about how messed up I was. "Get YOUR priorities straight," I told myself. "Soon I will be out of here and out of their lives."

There was that left ear voice. *"Hey, Toots! Enough now. You did good."* What's up with that freakin' voice in my left ear anyway?

Mom cautioned me, "Don't say anything else. Just get him a ticket. Now go to your room."

I managed one sullen word as I slammed my bedroom door "Oh, Frackensmacken!" That was as close to swearing as I would dare.

I stood at my bedroom window staring out at the picnic table. Just staring. I didn't cry, I didn't even feel disappointed. I was determined, absolutely determined, not to let "that man" keep affecting my life. I could graduate without his presence or him showing pride in my accomplishments. To him I was a failure; nothing I did was good enough for him. That was his problem, not mine. I was graduating for me, just for me. I earned my graduation with my persistent drive. I achieved success even when Dad didn't believe in me.

Mom knocked gently on my door which jarred me out of my innermost thoughts.

Dad was absolutely not going to get to me. Through my closed bedroom door I said, "I'm fine, Mom. Really, I'm fine." And I was.

I didn't want to be bothered. Denial of my feelings reached its peak. I was so ready to escape this family, but I planned to continue living at home when I went to MATC in fall. Lack of money to move out on my own and go to nursing school at the same time kept me imprisoned.

After the graduation ceremony, where I smiled so much my face hurt, Mom told me that Dad left his Masonic meeting and showed up just in time to see me walk across the stage to be handed my high school diploma. Then he left and returned to his meeting. I never saw him at graduation and in my heart I don't really believe he showed up. I smiled anyway. I had graduated high school at age sixteen!

My parents gave me a three-piece set of blue American Touristor luggage for my graduation present. I had never needed luggage in my life. Mom and Dad both received sets of luggage from their parents for high school graduation. Therefore, luggage was an appropriate, although useless, graduation gift. I wasn't going to travel anywhere. I used the luggage for storing off-season clothing.

After graduation, I worked full-time for ten weeks as a summer employee at the telephone company. My job in the teletype area was to "dead file" completed work orders. I was bored. However, that job was a learning experience and confirmed that I preferred to work with people. I enjoyed talking with my co-workers and I was grateful for their candid and sometimes very direct conversations. The most important thing I learned that summer was that I needed to do whatever felt right for me. Not for anyone else.

John showed up at the house on my seventeenth birthday. I talked with him through the screen door. I did not let him come in. I was busy. It was my birthday and I intended to celebrate with Grandma Lucille, Grandpa Ray and Grandpa Al.

Well, that "go away" message to John didn't turn out so well. He was in the Air Force and he was very persistent in trying to get my attention when he was home on military leave. We dated on and off the summer after my high school graduation.

The first day of college in the first hour of anatomy and physiology class I experienced a sudden onset of nausea and I ran into the hallway gasping for fresh air. Was it the smell from the anatomy lab? Nerves on my first day? Or what?

Section Six

■ Lessons Learned

Chapter 1: When looking for treasures in the attic do not snoop

Chapter 2: Romantic stories offer a nice beginning

Chapter 3: Keep Betsy-Wetsy doll close by at all times

Chapter 4: Do not jump off a chair holding a glass salt shaker

Chapter 5: Wear boots to keep shoes lasting longer

Chapter 6: Dance lessons not church choir

Chapter 7: Do not sleep on top bunks in a sleeping bag

Chapter 8: Pulled out permanent teeth will never grow back

Chapter 9: Brain in gear before mouth in action

Chapter 10: Black and white saddle shoes – never again

Chapter 11: Vote for your favorite Beatles song, no matter what

Chapter 12: Blue loafers-the best

Chapter 13: Keep on running!

Chapter 14: Sewing creates custom clothes

Chapter 15: Keep homework away from Dad

Chapter 16: Do not steal Dad's class ring to show off at school

Chapter 17: Do not act like a "tramp"(What's a tramp?)

Chapter 18: To be alone and feel a bit happy, stay in bedroom

Chapter 19: How not to behave, learned from Job's Daughters

Chapter 20: Summer school and volunteering at Home for Aged changed everything

Chapter 21: Don't take the Princess telephone extension out of parents' bedroom

Chapter 22: Do not skip school

Chapter 23: Do not disconnect the speedometer cable

Chapter 24: Don't drink booze

Chapter 25: Once again, DO NOT skip school

Chapter 26: Study Halls are unnecessary

Chapter 27: Pay your own way through college

Chapter 28: Persistence achieves high school graduation

Afterword

Dear Reader,

It is important to know that each of us has lessons we learn on our life path. Some lessons are buried deep. Unless one goes deep within, a great lesson may pass through your life without your awareness. The most significant lesson I learned while writing Zero to Seventeen was that I remembered finding Dad's high school class ring. I was not aware how deeply I was affected by his ring and everything the year 1953 represented.

When I remembered I had found the ring, it was an immediate "ah-ha" moment. I became aware how this event drove my behavior. I began to understand the angst I carried. The ring shattered my life as I knew it. As continued understanding melded with rising emotions I was able to release the angst and carry on. If I had not started writing down my memories, I would not have taken the path that uncovered "the ring." I am grateful that I followed this path.

With love and light-

Namasté

SR

Printed in the United States
By Bookmasters